IMAGES
of America

AROUND
OSWEGATCHIE

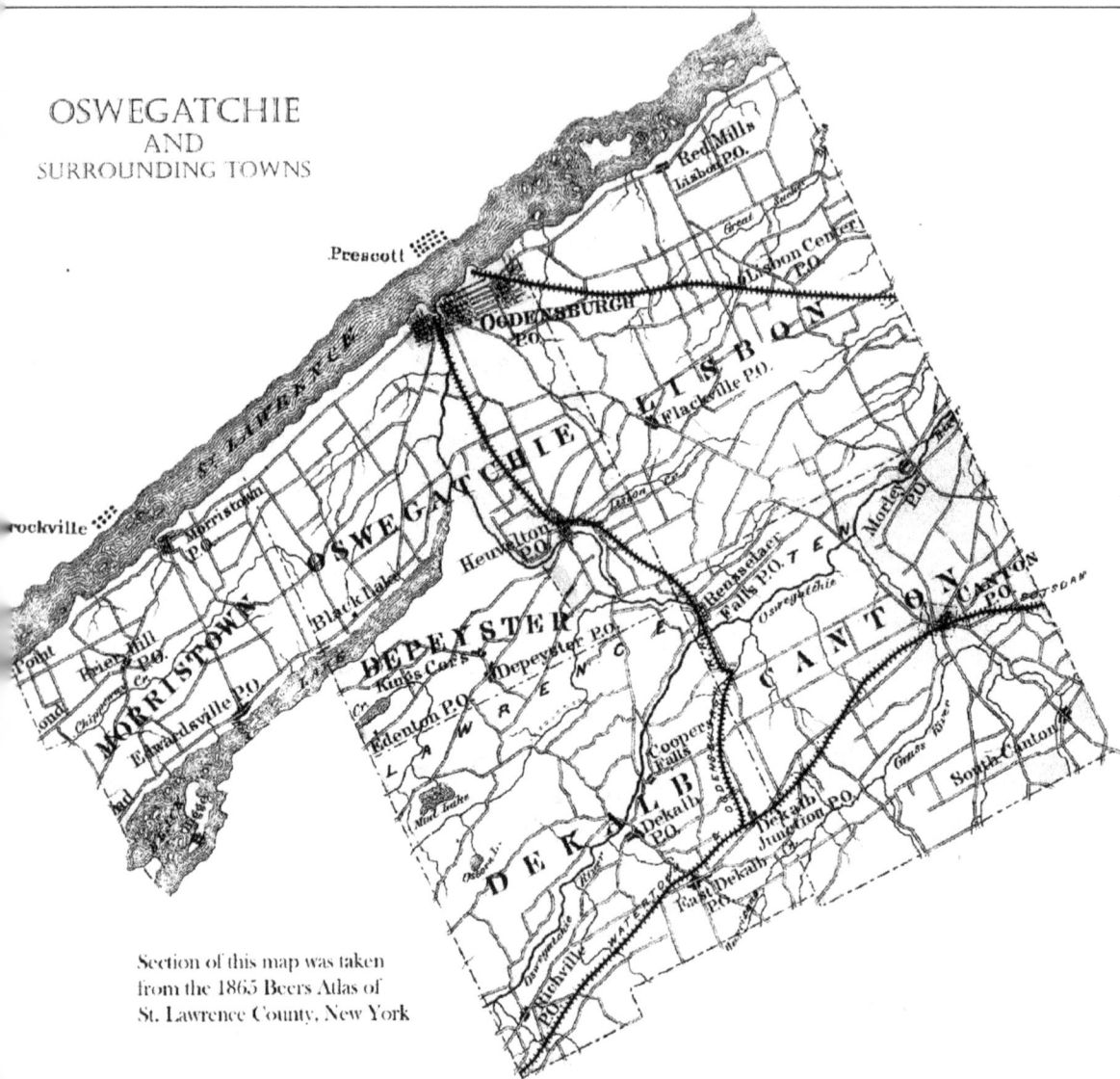

OSWEGATCHIE
AND
SURROUNDING TOWNS

Section of this map was taken
from the 1865 Beers Atlas of
St. Lawrence County, New York

AROUND OSWEGATCHIE. This northern section of St. Lawrence County is primarily agrarian, with small industrial concerns scattered throughout the area. In its heyday, most of the industry was concentrated around the city of Ogdensburg, which to this day still remains the only American city on the St. Lawrence River. Almost every community had cheese plants, blacksmith shops, general stores, inns, and hotels as well as one-room schoolhouses scattered throughout the area. One state report in 1845 indicated that there were 329 schools in St. Lawrence County, and almost all were within walking distance from most farms. This area has made great contributions to the world of art, politics, and education as well as numerous agrarian contributions related to the development of new breeds of animals and plants species and farming machinery. (Author's collection.)

IMAGES

of America

AROUND
OSWEGATCHIE

David E. Martin

ARCADIA
PUBLISHING

Library of Congress Catalog Card Number: 2005924383

For all general information contact Arcadia Publishing at:
Telephone 843-853-2070
Fax 843-853-0044
E-mail sales@arcadiapublishing.com
For customer service and orders:
Toll-Free 1-888-313-2665

Visit us on the Internet at www.arcadiapublishing.com

THE VANDEN HEUVEL GRISTMILL. Built in 1826, this was one of the largest gristmills located on the Oswegatchie River for many miles above and below the village of Heuvel (previously known as Fordsburg). The mill was operated by Alpheus Wright for Jacob A. Vanden Heuvel. Attached to the mill was a distillery and carding works. Also attached to the mill was a sawmill capable of producing large quantities of finished lumber for the general market. The distillery was later purchased by Nathan Ford Griffin and converted to a tannery. (Courtesy Town of Oswegatchie Historian.)

CONTENTS

ACKNOWLEDGMENTS

I would like to thank the following people for their assistance and cooperation in the compilation of this book: Trent Trulock, administrative director of the St. Lawrence County Historical Association; JeanMarie Martello, archives manager of the St. Lawrence County Historical Association; Linda Marshall, Town of Oswegatchie-Heuvelton historian; Marilyn Geddis, Town of Oswegatchie-Heuvelton deputy historian; Nancy LaFaver, Town of Lisbon historian; Sharon Murdock, Town of DePeyster historian; Mimi Barr, Village of Rensselaer Falls historian; and Robert G. Poor, Village of Rensselaer Falls deputy historian.

I would also like to thank the following people who contributed images from their private collections: Judy Skamperie, Robert Havens, Verna Hutchinson, Nancy LaFaver, Sharon Murdock, Fran Doyle, Eugene Jones, Cathy and Mark Rusgrove, Marjorie Rock, Pat Fields, Ed Night, Mary Lou Rupp, and Faye Witherell White.

INTRODUCTION

In the early 1600s, the French began to explore the northern coast of what is now America, searching for a northwest passage to Asia. After numerous expeditions, it became apparent that there was no route to Asia via the New World and that no gold was to be found to fill the coffers of the king of France. But what did not go unnoticed was the endless forest of hardwoods that covered the land and the seemingly limitless quantity of fur pelts to be had for the European market. It was not long before other countries became aware of the New World and wanted their share of the bounty. The king of England felt that the discoveries of Sebastian Cabot, the first man to sail up the Mississippi River, gave England rightful claim to all territories in the New World, including land already occupied by France. Before long, the French and British were locked into a state of continuous conflict known as the French and Indian Wars, which lasted from 1689 until 1763. As a result of the Treaty of Paris, the French were finally forced to relinquish all claims to territory in the Americas. The British controlled all of the Northern Territories and remained from August 25, 1760, through June 1, 1796.

The British met little or no resistance from the fledgling United States, which was expending most of its resources with the formation of a new government. The British remained in northern New York for almost 20 years, illegally cutting the best timber and harvesting fur pelts from the great forests and shipping them to Montreal for the British market. They finally left in 1796 with the proclamation of Jay's Treaty, in which they also relinquished all rights to the land.

The New York State legislature now opened the northern sections of the state for settlement and established 10 townships of approximately 64,000 acres each. These townships were further divided into smaller parcels to make them affordable and thus encourage settlers to move into the area, clear the land, and establish new communities. To further encourage settlement, land in each township was set aside to be used specifically for the construction of schools and for religious purposes.

The original 10 towns were Louisville, Stockholm, Potsdam, Madrid, Lisbon, Canton, DeKalb, Oswegatchie, Hague (now Hammond), and Cambray (now Gouverneur). With the passing of time, many of these original towns were further subdivided into smaller townships in order to conduct business without having to travel long distances to do so.

The majority of the original 10 towns were purchased by a wealthy land speculator from New York City by the name of Alexander Macomb. He acquired the land under somewhat questionable circumstances and was soon forced to sell his holdings to other speculators. Samuel Ogden, another speculator from New York City purchased most of the town of Oswegatchie along with surrounding areas. He sent his land agent, Nathan Ford, to divide and sell the land to settlers. Ford also purchased large areas of land for himself for future dealings.

The town of Lisbon was organized in 1801. Located in the northern section of St. Lawrence County along the St. Lawrence River, Lisbon contains some of the finest farmland in the county.

The town of Oswegatchie was organized in 1802. Oswegatchie contained the village of Ogdensburg, which was the county seat for St. Lawrence County. Many felt that the village was too far from much of the county, so the seat was moved to Canton in 1830.

Hague (now Morristown) was formed on March 27, 1821. The name may have come from the Gouverneur Morris family, who were some of the area's original landowners, or the family of David Ford, who were from Morristown, New Jersey.

The town of DePeyster was organized on March 24, 1825. A substantial portion of the land was taken from the town of Oswegatchie, while the remainder of the land was taken from the town of DeKalb.

Most of the small towns and villages throughout New York and the rest of the country were too small to get much attention by themselves, but these communities have much to offer and have played important roles in the development of the country. From communities such as these have come some of the greatest soldiers, politicians, doctors, inventors, industrialists, and artists of our time. People such as these have had a major effect on the country and even the world. It seems only fitting that we mention a few of the towns here, for they, like so many other places, have contributed much and will continue to do so in the future.

One

OSWEGATCHIE

LISBON STREET. This is the intersection of State and Lisbon Streets. Lisbon Street provided a direct route to the hamlet of Flackville and the town and village of Lisbon. These early roads were primarily corduroy and plank roads. They were made into toll roads to finance their constant need for repair. Here we can see the post office on the right and the Presbyterian church farther down on the left side of the street. (Courtesy St. Lawrence County Historical Association.)

ANNETTE AND WATER STREETS. This view is looking north across the Oswegatchie River at the intersection of Annette Street. The house to the left is the Snyder House. According to the 1865 Beers atlas of St. Lawrence County, the house on the right was the property of John Pickens, and the house to the far right was the home of N. F. Griffin. In the center behind the two white houses can be seen the rear of the Methodist Episcopal church. (Courtesy St. Lawrence County Historical Association.)

CHARLES SNYDER HOUSE. This house was built in 1899 at the intersection of Annette and Water Streets by Charles Snyder and his wife, Lura Coffin. In its later years, the house became the property of the Richardson family. Over the years, the interior of the house had been subdivided into a number of apartments. The house still stands today, but it is a shadow of the stately mansion it once was. (Courtesy Town of Oswegatchie Historian.)

POLITICAL BANNER. Hanging over the intersection of State and Lisbon Streets is a banner for the presidential election in 1916. Charles Evan Hughes ran for president, and Charles Warren Fairbanks ran for vice president. Both candidates, however, were defeated by Woodrow Wilson at the polls. Although these small communities were somewhat isolated from the major urban centers, they managed to keep abreast of national affairs. (Courtesy Town of Oswegatchie Historian.)

BUSINESS SECTION. The main focal point of activity in Heuvelton was the train station. This view from the platform shows area locals flocking to town to conduct business, send goods away on the train, or pick up goods at the station. The railway kept the community well supplied throughout the year, and the main street was lined with many stores and shops. (Courtesy Town of Oswegatchie Historian.)

WATER STREET. This view is looking east on Water Street. The street follows the Oswegatchie River to the village limits, and the road continues on to the village of Rensselaer Falls. The man in the buggy is probably going to or coming from the milk plant or transfer station, as the container in the back of the buggy is the type used to carry milk. The man with the sawhorse is probably going to cut firewood. (Courtesy St. Lawrence County Historical Association.)

WASHINGTON STREET. Looking east on Washington Street, we see a few of the fine homes present in Heuvelton. The fourth building from the left is the Union Free School, built in 1874 and razed in 1954. A new school was built in this same location and still stands today. Between the third house from the left and the school was a cemetery that had been moved to a new location a few blocks away to allow for the expansion of the new school. (Courtesy St. Lawrence County Historical Association.)

THE SNYDER HOUSE. This popular hotel was built and operated by John Snyder. The hotel was famous for its "floating" dance floor, which was the only one of its kind in the North Country. The hotel was also famous for the New Year's dances held there each year. The Snyder House offered the finest accommodations for businessmen and travelers alike, and there was a large carriage house in the back to provide livery services. (Courtesy Town of Oswegatchie Historian.)

BRECKENRIDGE AND SNYDER. This building stood on the corner of Union and State Streets on the south side of the bridge in the village of Heuvelton. Here could be purchased McCormick harvesting machinery, crockery, glassware, tools needed on the farm, and items for the home. Attached to the store is the Snyder House. These two buildings stood where the present firehouse stands today. (Courtesy Town of Oswegatchie Historian.)

ADRIAN MEAT MARKET. Warner B. Adrian stands in the doorway to his butcher shop on State Street. Many of the citizens of the village were also members of the Heuvelton Volunteer Fire Company, which was organized on June 28, 1921. When the alarm was given, all members of the bucket brigade, as well as any able-bodied men in the area, would immediately respond to the fire. (Courtesy Town of Oswegatchie Historian.)

MEAT MARKET. This meat market was located on State Street in the village of Heuvelton. Standing behind the counter is Warner Adrain, the butcher. Hanging on the back wall is the saw used to cut through bone while butchering meat. Most farmers still produced most of their meat and poultry, but the village residents now walked to the market each day for fresh meat. (Courtesy Town of Oswegatchie Historian.)

THE VAN HEUVEL HOUSE. By 1900, Heuvelton was a busy commercial and agricultural community requiring facilities for itinerate businessmen and visitors. The Van Heuvel House (named after the town founder, Jacob A. Van Heuvel) was built around 1846. In 1864, it was one of three hotels in Heuvelton. In its later years, Warner Adrian was the owner and lived with his family in the small house next to the hotel. The structure stood on the corner of State and Lisbon Streets until it was razed in 1959. (Courtesy Town of Oswegatchie Historian.)

THE VAN HEUVEL HOUSE LOBBY. The lobby was equipped with numerous chairs and spittoons, providing a place for the men to meet, smoke their cigars, and play cards. Notice the well-stocked variety of cigars in the display case. Cigars were shipped in on the railroad from all over the country and Europe, as well as some from Ogdensburg, which had several cigar manufacturers in the city. The man wearing the tie is the owner, Gene Gray, and the other man is believed to be Frank George, a member of the hotel staff. (Courtesy Town of Oswegatchie Historian.)

GENERAL STORE. This stone building, located just over the bridge on State Street, was built in 1853 by Nathan Ford Giffin. Nathan sold boots, shoes, harnesses, and groceries. He also operated a tannery. In 1887, he sold the property to George C. McFadden and Charles P. Anderson, who converted the building into a gristmill and feed store. Standing here are, from left to right, John Crawford Jr., Charles P. Anderson, Harlan Smithers, and William Smith. (Courtesy Town of Oswegatchie Historian.)

STATE STREET, LOOKING NORTH. This view looks up the street toward the railroad depot. The highest building on the left is the Van Heuvel House. To the immediate right is the Pickens block, and the tiny building next to it is a barbershop. Mrs. Smithers's meat market is followed by what appears to be a billiard parlor and then a furniture store. The post office is at the top of the hill near the New York Central railroad tracks. (Courtesy Town of Oswegatchie Historian.)

16

PICKENS STORE. This store, located on the corner of State and Water Streets, was built by John Pickens in 1858. It proved to be a successful enterprise and continued for many years. When opened, the building housed a grocery store, a dry goods store, a shoe store, and a grain store. Through the years, the building had many other stores within its walls. The structure still stands today after being stabilized and renovated. It will soon be the new home of the Heuvelton Historical Association. (Courtesy Town of Oswegatchie Historian.)

THE PRESTON BLOCK. This building was located at the southeast corner of State Street and Riverside Drive. It housed the Preston Store as well as a small theater and the Preston Undertaking Service. Originally established by Claude L. Preston, the business was continued by his son Claude H. Preston and his wife. The store operated until 1947. The building was torn down in the early 1960s, and a small building was built on that location to house the post office. (Courtesy Town of Oswegatchie Historian.)

GEORGE HAYDON FEED STORE. The Haydon feed store was located in the center of State Street on the west side of the street. Haydon was a dealer in flour, feed, groceries, and other general goods. The milk delivery is from Pleasant View Farms. The sign on the wagon indicates that the milk is sanitized, showing that milk is now pasteurized before being sold to the public. There were no playgrounds, so children made the best of what was available. In the winter months, they would careen down the boardwalks on their sleds, causing havoc among the pedestrians. (Courtesy St. Lawrence County Historical Association.)

SMOKE CLUB. This image represents a group of men who wanted in some way to assist our soldiers serving overseas during World War II. They met at the Van Heuvel House and in the barn behind the hotel. They held dances in the town hall to raise money in order to purchase Series E government bonds, showing their support for the service men from the area. Here we see many of the bonds in display behind the bar in the Van Heuvel House. The man on the left is Gene Gray, and on the right is Leroy (Sandy) Manfred. (Courtesy Town of Oswegatchie Historian.)

FIRST NATIONAL BANK. The First National Bank of Heuvelton was established in 1913. Before that time, it was necessary to go to Ogdensburg, a trip that often required considerable time and effort, traveling over unpaved roads, through mud, and sometimes through heavy snow. William H. McCadam was the first president, and Everett H. Fletcher was the first vice president. Located on the corner of Lisbon and State Streets, the bank still stands today. (Courtesy Town of Oswegatchie Historian.)

FIRST NATIONAL BANK OF HEUVELTON. From the onset, it was questionable if a bank would survive in such a small community, but the bank was soon shown to be a great success. Shown here are, from left to right, Charles S. Bourdon, Stanley Lake, and Forrest Wood. In 1963, the bank merged with the St. Lawrence County National Bank. To this day, it is a thriving enterprise in the town of Oswegatchie. (Courtesy Town of Oswegatchie Historian.)

LUMBERMILL. This lumbermill, located on the Oswegatchie River, was typical for the day. Logs were floated down the river to the mill as individual logs or bound into tight rafts containing thousands of logs, depending on the level of the tide. At the mill, the logs were winched up a ramp into the saw blades, where the logs were squared off and then cut into boards. The sawdust was carried away by a chain conveyor and retained for other uses. (Courtesy Town of Oswegatchie Historian.)

SHOVELING SAWDUST. A major by-product of the lumber industry is sawdust. Here we see men shoveling sawdust into wagons. Sawdust was needed to pack around blocks of ice in homes and icehouses. An excellent insulator, sawdust prevented ice from melting during the warmest summer months, making yearlong refrigeration possible. Having many uses, sawdust was also used for animal bedding and insulating homes by packing it into dead air spaces in the walls. (Courtesy Town of Oswegatchie Historian.)

SAWMILL INTERIOR. This mill was designed to produce large quantities of construction lumber in a short period of time. Notice that the saw is basically a large band saw with the blade having teeth on both sides. This allows the saw to make a cut with each pass of the lot carriage. Also note that two logs are mounted one above the other to allow both to be cut at the same time. (Courtesy St. Lawrence County Historical Association.)

LOGJAM. Oswegatchie and surrounding towns were heavily forested with numerous varieties of oak, maple, and other useful varieties of trees. The easiest way to move the logs to the mill was to float them down various rivers directly to the mills. In times of low water or if too many logs were rafted together, logs would snag on the bottom or fail to slide over dams, and thus logjams were created. Breaking up these logjams was a very dangerous task requiring great skill. A long pole called a pike was used to push and pry the logs apart. (Courtesy Town of Oswegatchie Historian.)

HERMAN MILLS CHEESE PLANT. This building was originally used as a gristmill and butter factory. It was purchased by James C. Birge and modified for cheese production. Birge ran the plant until 1894, when he sold it to William H. McCadam, who in turn ran the plant until 1896. The plant was then sold to A. B. Hargrave, who sold the mill in 1903 to Herman Mills. (Courtesy Town of Oswegatchie Historian.)

FLIGHT CHEESE FACTORY. This was the last of several small cheese factories scattered throughout the county. It was located on the Ogdensburg-Heuvelton Road and built in 1874 by Benjamin Flight. David Woods was the superintendent, and Wilber Harland was the cheese maker. The cheese process varied from one factory to another, as family recipes were often used. This created a large variety for the general market. (Courtesy Town of Oswegatchie Historian.)

DAM CONSTRUCTION. The first dam built on this section of the Oswegatchie River was constructed in the early 1800s by Jarius Remington, who was encouraged to come and settle in the area by Nathan Ford of Ogdensburg. Ford was acting as a land agent for Samuel Ogden, who wanted to see the area opened to settlers and a community built there. The dam was anchored to the bedrock on the bottom of the river and constructed of timber cribs filled with rocks. This dam, however, was not very high and thus did not have sufficient weight to hold it in place. Consequently, it was frequently in need of repair. (Courtesy Town of Oswegatchie Historian.)

DAM DESIGN. The design of this dam was pretty much a standard used throughout Europe at this time. The timber-framed cribs filled with rock provided adequate stability for higher dams, and they were usually heavy enough that they did not move, even during periods of high water. The dam had a timber deck that angled from the top of the dam to the river bottom in the rear of the dam. This deck would allow ice, logs, and debris to slide up and over the dam without creating jams. (Courtesy Town of Oswegatchie Historian.)

HEUVELTON DEPOT. The depot in Heuvelton was the major hub of commercial and agrarian activity for the entire Heuvelton area. With the mobility of the railroad, people could visit other communities without having to spend the entire day traveling. Shown standing at the depot are, from left to right, Harley Conklin, Robert Woodside, J. R. Humphrey, and Archie Elsworth (stationmaster from 1890 to 1928). (Courtesy Judy Skamperle.)

FIRST RAILROAD. The Rome, Watertown and Ogdensburg Railroad became the first line to pass through Heuvelton and the surrounding area. It was now possible for farmers to get their milk, butter, cheese, and poultry to larger markets. Between 1893 and 1928, Heuvelton was known as the world's largest dressed turkey market. It was not unusual to see 25 to 40 tons of turkeys shipped at one time, an agricultural boom that could only happen with the advent of the railroad. (Courtesy Town of Oswegatchie Historian.)

24

F. J. DUCETT GENERAL STORE. In 1912, Fred J. Ducett and his wife opened a general store in the stone building built by John Pickens in 1858. The Ducetts sold general merchandise until 1924, when they branched out, utilizing more of the building for other departments that sold footware, wallpaper, and paints. Both were active in the business until Mrs. Ducett died in 1951 and he died in 1962. (Courtesy Town of Oswegatchie Historian.)

DUCETT STORE. Orman and Earl took over the store run by their parents since 1912. They continued to operate the store until 1964, when they sold the building to Paul L. Wood, who operated a grocery store at that location under the name of Woods IGA. (Courtesy Town of Oswegatchie Historian.)

LAKE AND RIVER NAVIGATION. Commercial navigation first started on the Oswegatchie River and Black Lake around 1900. Some boats were either built in local communities such as Rossie, Heuvelton, or Edwardsville or dragged across land by oxen pulling the boats over rollers. Most commercial boats were steamers having flat bottoms to navigate in shallow waters and were either sternwheelers or sidewheelers. Here we see the sternwheeler *Oswegatchie* on Black Lake. (Courtesy St. Lawrence County Historical Association.)

STEAMER OSWEGATCHIE. The steamer *Oswegatchie* first took to the waters in 1905. For several years, it was a very profitable venture, hauling cargo and passengers. Cargo was often stacked on the upper deck, causing the steamer to be top-heavy. At one point, it was literally pushed over by high winds on Black Lake. The steamer was raised but never took to the waters again. (Courtesy Town of Oswegatchie Historian.)

26

THE PEAT DREDGE. A grandiose scheme to dredge peat from the bogs of Black Lake to be used for fuel ended in disaster for its investors. The dredge was built in Heuvelton, and the machinery was built in Ogdensburg. When towed to the lake, the dredge was unable to make sufficient fuel for its own boilers and was thus proven to be a failed concern. The dredge was anchored near the opening to Black Lake on September 21, 1908, when it caught fire and was destroyed, never to be rebuilt. (Courtesy Town of Oswegatchie Historian.)

TOWN OF HEUVELTON BASKETBALL TEAM. The town basketball team actively competed with other teams from the area. From 1914 to 1915, the Heuvelton team was known as the Crescents. The photograph shows, from left to right, the following: (first row) Leon Connolly and Clinton Connolly; (second row) Earl Goodison, Andre DeMott, and Raymond Goodison. (Courtesy St. Lawrence County Historical Association.)

27

EARLY SCHOOL. Among the first schools to be built in the village of Heuvelton was this one-story, two-room structure built on a lot provided by Jacob Vanden Heuvel. Located on what was then the corner of York and Washington Streets. This was one of two stone buildings built at that location and later became known as District No. 5. The stone schoolhouse was in continuous use until 1874, when it was replaced by a new timber-frame structure called the Union Free School. (Courtesy Town of Oswegatchie Historian.)

UNION FREE SCHOOL. This two-story frame structure was built on the same Washington Street location as the early stone school, known as District No. 5. At some point, considerable modifications had been made, and the new additions almost doubled the size of the school. The school continued to be used until 1954, when it was torn down to make room for the present structure. York Street terminated at the school, and the land was used for enlarging the school. (Courtesy Town of Oswegatchie Historian.)

28

GALILEE SCHOOL. This one-room structure was located near the Galilee Methodist Church. Also known as School No. 7, the Galilee School was one of two built on this location. It was one of numerous schools built locally so that children were within walking distance to school. Another school, School No. 11, stood at the intersection of Black Lake Road and Camp Road. Another was located at the intersection of Stone Church and Middle Roads. (Courtesy Town of Oswegatchie Historian.)

GRADUATION CLASS. This is a senior graduating class from the Union Free School in the village of Heuvelton. The date of the graduation is not known, but the names of the graduates are. From left to right are the following: (first row) Dave Bell, Delbert Hutchinson, Walter Fletcher, and Edgar Adrian; (second row) Mar Badger, Elsie Backus, Ethel McClellan, Doris Dollar, and Jane Ellisworth. (Courtesy Verna Hutchinson.)

GROVE HOTEL. The Grove Hotel was initially the home of John Pickens, a successful businessman in the village of Heuvelton who built the mansion in 1858. The Pickens family lived in the home until 1893. On January 26, 1896, the property was sold to John Trainor of Heuvelton, who leased it as a hotel. The building has since been used as apartments, a post office, and numerous other functions. It still stands today. (Courtesy St. Lawrence County Historical Association.)

BESSIE ABOTT. Bessie Abott and her twin sister Jessie were the daughters of John Pickins Jr. and his wife, Josephine Button. The twins were born in the family home built by John Pickins in 1858 on Water Street. Bessie married T. Waldo Story (the sculptor) and died at her home on Park Avenue in New York on February 10, 1919. Jessie married a prominent New York City physician, Dr. Henry H. Lyle. She died in New York in 1949. (Courtesy Town of Oswegatchie Historian.)

BESSIE ABOTT, OPERA STAR. Bessie and her twin sister Jessie began singing at an early age and were soon preforming song and dance in a vaudeville act. Bessie had a voice worth developing. She went to Paris, where she studied under Jean de Reszke. She made her debut at the Paris opera on December 9, 1901, as Juliette. After singing at the Paris opera, she returned to the United States a full-fledged prima donna, making her debut at the Metropolitan Opera House. Here we see her in the role of Maid Marion in the opera *Robin Hood*. (Courtesy Town of Oswegatchie Historian.)

EARLY SNOWPLOW. In the early days, there was no attempt to keep roads open during the winter. If snow was too deep for cutters, milk and other products were shipped by train. Roads were often closed all winter until the spring thaw. This old tractor was a vain attempt to keep the road open between Ogdensburg and Canton. (Courtesy St. Lawrence County Historical Association.)

METHODIST EPISCOPAL CHURCH. This beautiful brick structure was constructed to replace a wood-frame building destroyed by fire in 1933. Services were held above the Ducett store while the new church was being built. The brick church was completed in 1934, and a dedication ceremony was held in June of that year. A time capsule placed in the previous church was recovered by older members who remembered its placement in 1870, and the capsule was installed in the cornerstone of the new church. (Courtesy Verna Hutchinson.)

ST. RAPHAEL'S CATHOLIC CHURCH.
Originally built in 1829 by Jacob Vanden
Heuvel for use by the Episcopal Society, the
church was later used by the Universalists.
The church changed denominations again in
1881, when it was taken over by the Catholic
church that had been established in Heuvelton.
Through the years, the church underwent
many renovations, including the sale of a part
of its property to the town for the location of
the town hall. (Courtesy St. Lawrence County
Historical Association.)

THE PRESBYTERIAN CHURCH. This church was first used as a Congregational church, an offshoot from the Episcopal church. The building was completed and dedicated in 1844. In 1859, the church was again changed from Congregational to Presbyterian. The structure seen here was completed and dedicated on December 30, 1867, at this location on Lisbon Street. (Courtesy St. Lawrence County Historical Association.)

THE LAST COVERED BRIDGE. In 1802, a log bridge was built across the Oswegatchie River in what is now Heuvelton. At that time, the village was known as Fordsburg, after landowner Nathan Ford, who encouraged many settlers to come and settle in this area. This bridge was replaced by two covered bridges on State Street. The covered bridge pictured here was the last covered bridge to cross the river at Heuvelton. (Courtesy St. Lawrence County Historical Association.)

THE NEW IRON BRIDGE. This iron-truss bridge was constructed in 1875. The covered bridges required considerable maintenance. They were usually built too close to the water, which often led to their being washed away by high water in the spring. The iron-truss bridge, however, could be built to any height and could span greater distances. This new construction eliminated the need for a center support in the river, which could impede the flow of water and ice. (Courtesy St. Lawrence County Historical Association.)

CONCRETE BRIDGE. The concrete bridge was built in 1916 to replace the iron truss that was now too narrow and suffering from age and overuse. A new bridge was needed that could support heavier loads and had a smoother deck, which would be easier on vehicular traffic. Through the years, a number of changes and repairs have been made to this bridge, but it is still in use today. (Courtesy St. Lawrence County Historical Association.)

MORNING RITUAL. More milk is produced in the town of Oswegatchie than any other product. Some of this milk is used for the home manufacture of butter, but most of it is used to make cheese. Each morning after milking their cows, the farmers take their milk in large milk cans (seen here in the wagons) to the cheese plant for processing into cheese. Here we see the farmers lined up on the corner of State and Union Streets. (Courtesy Town of Oswegatchie Historian.)

STATE STREET SOUTH. Looking south on State Street, this view shows Stewart Bro's Beauty and Barber Supply Company, a diner, the W. B. Adrian meat market, the Brandy drugstore, and Nugent's. (Courtesy St. Lawrence County Historical Association.)

STATE STREET NORTH. Visible in this view looking north up State Street are Nugent's and the Brandy drugstore on the left side of the street. At the far end of the street is the Van Heuvel House. Beyond that, just out of sight, are the New York Central train station and, just over the tracks, the St. Lawrence County National Bank. (Courtesy Town of Oswegatchie Historian.)

SKY VIEW, EAST. This view shows the Oswegatchie River running through the village of Heuvelton. The river has been the lifeblood of numerous communities that developed along its banks ever since the county was first developed. The river originates from Cranberry Lake in the Adirondack Mountains, meanders for 120 miles through the county, and empties into the St. Lawrence River at Ogdensburg. Also seen here are the latest concrete bridge and the Niagara Mohawk Power Dam. Electricity first came to the area in 1906, when a dynamo was installed at a mill in Millville, marking the start of a new era. (Courtesy St. Lawrence County Historical Association.)

SKY VIEW, NORTH. In this view looking north, State Street bisects the village of Heuvelton. Entering and leaving the village, the road becomes Route 812, leading to Ogdensburg in the north and connecting to Route 11 and the village of Governeur in the south. (Courtesy St. Lawrence County Historical Association.)

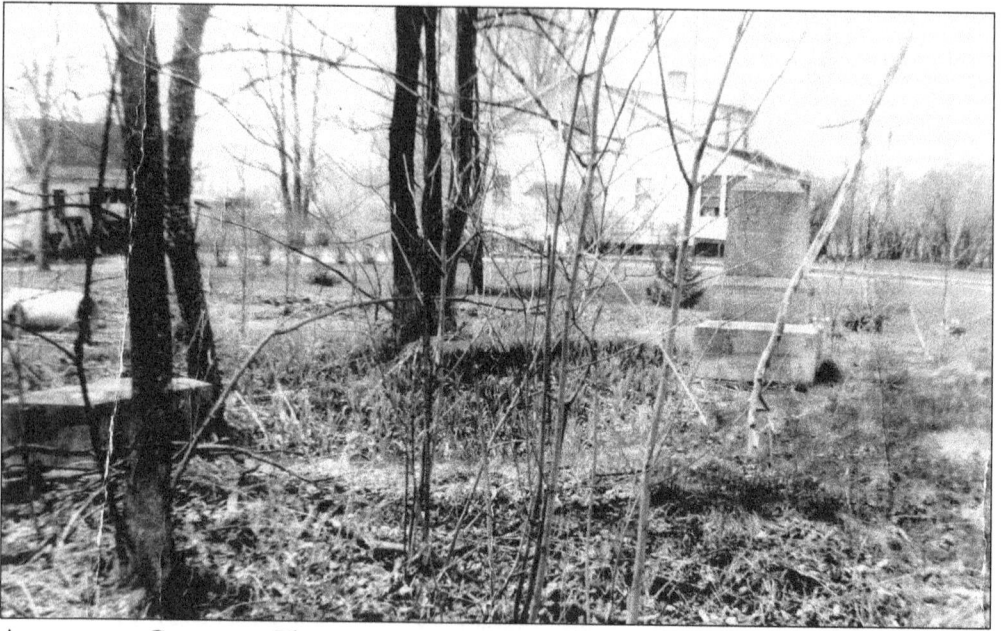

ABANDONED CEMETERY. This is one of the many abandoned cemeteries located throughout St. Lawrence County. The cemetery was located next to St. John's Hospital, across from the Notre Dame cemetery, on old county Route 6 (now known as Black Lake Road). The cemetery was abandoned in the early 1920s, and the bodies were moved across the road to the Notre Dame cemetery. (Courtesy Town of Oswegatchie Historian.)

HEUVELTON'S FIRST CEMETERY. The first cemetery in Heuvelton was located to the right of this house at 9 Washington Street, now 77 Washington Street. York Street continued on past the school, placing the cemetery on the corner of Washington and York Streets. Today, located on the old cemetery lot, is the Town of Heuvelton water tower and the playground next to the public school. (Courtesy Robert Havens.)

THE NEW VILLAGE CEMETERY. On September 8, 1868, eight acres of land were purchased from the Ridge Farm on Rensselaer Road at a cost of $100 to $150 per acre. Individual lots were sold for $15 apiece. The vault was built in 1931. Still in use today, the cemetery has a large stand of stately oak and maple trees scattered throughout the area. (Courtesy Town of Oswegatchie Historian.)

UPPER STATE STREET. The brick home shown here on the left was originally built by Rawlings Webster and later occupied by William Prouse, Grosvenor T. Howard, and Frank Rounds. The home was eventually razed, and in July 1948, construction was started at this location for the new village library. (Courtesy Town of Oswegatchie Historian.)

WINONA ALLEN MEMORIAL LIBRARY. On the corner of Clinton and State Streets sits the new Winona Allen Memorial Library. In 1939, Winona Allen left a sum of money for the specific purpose of building a new library for the village. She had a deep concern for anything that might be of benefit to the village. Among other interested parties who left money for the library were Carlos S. Blood, W. Palmer Smith, and Henry Ferris. (Courtesy Town of Oswegatchie Historian.)

TOWN HALL. All governmental functions for the city of Ogdensburg and the town of Oswegatchie were conducted in Ogdensburg. After Oswegatchie separated from Ogdensburg, it became necessary to construct facilities so that Oswegatchie could conduct its own business. The town built the town hall as well as housing for the fire department in the same building in Heuvelton. Although the fire department has moved, town business is still conducted in this building. (Courtesy Town of Oswegatchie Historian.)

MECHANICS BAND. The brass band was a popular form of entertainment before the era of television. Here is an image of the Mechanics Band with the Pickens residence in the background. From left to right are O. C. Goodenough, Robert Johnson, Lewis Simmons, James Bell, Homer Furness, Frank Johnson, Walter Millard, ? Anderson, John Baker, Homer Johnson, George McFadden, William Popple, Charles Flack, Fred Lanning, and Foster Johnson. (Courtesy St. Lawrence County Historical Association.)

MILLINERY SHOP. This shop appears approximately in the center of the business block on State Street in the village of Heuvelton. The building was built by George Seaman and later known as the Lanning House. It was demolished by Henry Ferris in the fall of 1912. In the spring of 1913, he built a new store that was 60 by 40 feet. The building today is known as Doug's Tavern. (Courtesy Town of Oswegatchie Historian.)

BRIDGE REPLACEMENT. The iron-truss bridge built in 1875 was replaced in 1916 by a concrete structure. With the advent of steel reinforcement rods and better formulas for the concrete mix, more massive and sturdier structures could be built more economically. Here the forms are under construction for the deck of the new bridge. (Courtesy Town of Oswegatchie Historian.)

FROZEN OSWEGATCHIE. As usual, the Oswegatchie River freezes over each year with ice that may be 12 inches or more in thickness. In the spring, the ice breaks up and flows rapidly down the river with the spring floods. It is easy to see how the ice could have done so much damage to shoreline structures and older bridges made of wood. This photograph was taken from the iron-truss bridge before Niagara Mohawk built the new power dam, which provided power and lights to much of the surrounding community. (Courtesy Town of Oswegatchie Historian.)

POST OFFICE. These men are standing in front of the post office, located at the corner of State and Lisbon Streets. From left to right are Alex McClelland, William McFadden, Newton Connolly, Norman Smith (the postmaster), and a Mr. Allison. (Courtesy Town of Oswegatchie Historian.)

SCHOOLHOUSE GATHERING. During the latter half of the 1800s, the bicycle was a major mode of local transportation. Bicycle clubs formed all over the country, often riding from town to town in large groups. This group of people on the steps of the Union Free School may be a bicycle club or a religious organization. (Courtesy Town of Oswegatchie Historian.)

LOG CABIN. When the first settlers came to this area, they built their homes out of what was available. A forested area was almost always nearby, so logs were usually the building material of choice. Nathan Ford built three log cabins in 1802 to provide housing for workers and to encourage settlers to come to the area. This log cabin was located between Ogdensburg and Canton. (Courtesy St. Lawrence County Historical Association.)

THE SPILE BRIDGE. This old King Bridge spans the mouth of Black Lake, where it empties into the Oswegatchie River, and connected the towns of Oswegatchie and DePeyster. The bridge originally consisted of five spans built in 1874 at Ogdensburg to replace an original bridge made of wood (hemlock). The King Bridge Company, builders of iron bridges, was founded by George King of King's Corners in DePeyster. (Courtesy Town of DePeyster Historian.)

Two

DePeyster

LOCAL BLACKSMITH SHOP. In the late 1800s, there were probably more horses than people in DePeyster. In 1865, there were two such shops in DePeyster. When tools were broken or new parts were needed for machinery, they were often fixed or made by the local blacksmith. Here we see Purley A. Bogardus in his shop. He was a well-known blacksmith in DePeyster for many years. He was born in 1879 and died in 1962. He and his wife lived above the blacksmith shop. (Courtesy Town of DePeyster Historian.)

FREDERIC DEPEYSTER. The town of DePeyster was formed in 1825 by portioning sections of land from the towns of Oswegatchie and DeKalb. Frederic DePeyster owned a large section of the land taken from the town of DeKalb. The town opted to take the name of DePeyster after an 800-pound bell was donated to the town in his name by his son on July 4, 1840. (Courtesy Town of DePeyster Historian.)

MAIN STREET, DEPEYSTER. Visible in this post-1880s view of Main Street in DePeyster are, from left to right, the J. D. Wilson store, the James Conklin blacksmith shop, the Mason House, and the Congregational church. It appears as though the Conklin shop is being torn down to make room for a new structure. (Courtesy St. Lawrence County Historical Association.)

HON. SMITH STILWELL. In 1801, Smith Stilwell purchased a piece of land in the town of Oswegatchie that later became part of DePeyster, and he established a farm on the property. He was appointed associate judge of the common pleas in 1823 and preformed his duties to the highest expectations of the community. He was also the first town supervisor from 1825 to 1829 and the first postmaster in 1827. He was collector of the port of Ogdensburg in 1836 and a member of the assembly in 1851 and 1852. (Courtesy Town of DePeyster Historian.)

TURKEY DAY. Nearly every farmer raised a flock of turkeys, which were taken to Heuvelton twice a year and then put on the train for New York City or Boston. Some 20 to 40 tons of birds were shipped at a time, making turkey growing a very successful agricultural product along with butter and cheese. (Courtesy Town of DePeyster Historian.)

JAMES J. MASON. A citizen of DePeyster for many years, James Mason was apparently the second owner of the Mason House. In 1832, he was elected town clerk of the town of DePeyster and served in that capacity for eight years. (Courtesy Town of DePeyster Historian.)

THE MASON HOUSE. The Mason House was somewhat centrally located in the village of DePeyster. The first recorded owners were Abel Mason and his wife, Puah. At the time this photograph was taken, James J. Mason was the proprietor. The hotel was used for holding numerous public functions, including dances and meetings. Over the years, the building has been modified several times, but it still stands today. (Courtesy Town of DePeyster Historian.)

M. C. MASON GENERAL STORE. This store was located in the village of DePeyster. When M. C. Mason was a young man, G. H. Fletham ran the store while Mason served as an employee. The building was destroyed by fire on January 3, 1933, and then rebuilt. At a later date, the store was managed by E. E. Todd & Son. (Courtesy Town of DePeyster Historian.)

MASON GENERAL STORE. The first telephone to be installed in the town of DePeyster was installed in the Mason store. M. C. Mason was a town supervisor from 1883 until 1888. He was known for his fair dealing and honesty. He sold groceries, clothing, hardware, and oil in one side of the building and lived in the other. Mason died in 1925. (Courtesy Town of DePeyster Historian.)

JOHN D. WILSON. John Wilson was in business in the same location in DePeyster for more than 50 years. He started with a wholesale and retail meat market and branched out into a line of groceries in 1881. Some of the items he carried were gates, matches, birdseed, bath bricks, scouring bricks for steel table knives, 50-gallon barrels of syrup or molasses, pails of chewing tobacco, and cases of plug tobacco. Wilson is pictured standing outside the store next to a fuel pump. (Courtesy Town of DePeyster Historian.)

WILSON STORE AND HOME. John D. Wilson and his wife, Jennie Humphrey, lived in one end of the store. The original building had apartments at both ends of the building, with the store in the middle and a butcher shop in the back. Wilson converted one of the apartments into store space and lived in the other. Being centrally located in the village made it convenient for most residents to shop there. In addition, there was plenty of room in front of the store for horses and buggies. (Courtesy Town of DePeyster Historian.)

ALONZO THORNTON. Alonzo Thornton was born on November 29, 1832, in the village of DePeyster. In 1855, he married Mary Elizabeth Austin, the daughter of Gouverneur Morris Austin. They had six children, all of whom were successful in their life endeavors. Alonzo spent most of his life in the lumber industry and started his first mill at Mud Lake. When he died in 1931 at the age of 98, he was one of the oldest residents in St. Lawrence County. (Courtesy Town of DePeyster Historian.)

GRACE WITHERELL. Grace was born on December 18, 1906. She is seen here standing on the front porch of the home that she lived in for all but 12 of her 90 years of life in DePeyster. She was the daughter of Charles and Luda Witherell. She taught school at the Flat Rock and East Road schools in DePeyster. She married Wilbert Parish, also of DePeyster, and raised her seven children in the home where she was born. Grace started the first 4-H Club in DePeyster. She was very active in the Methodist church and the Grange on the local, county, and state levels. (Courtesy Sharon Murdock.)

GIFFIN HOME. This house next to the Giffin Cheese Factory was built at the end of the 19th century. The foundation was built using stone taken from an old church that stood in the area of the present village park. Newton Young was the carpenter in charge of building the Giffin house. Cheese making was discontinued in 1940, and the factory was modified for the production of butter. (Courtesy Town of DePeyster Historian.)

GIFFIN FACTORY. This cheese factory was located on Plympton Road in DePeyster and was the successor to the cheese factory, which was located between the village of DePeyster and Kokomo Corners. During the season of 1861, a total of 2,040,161 pounds of milk were delivered to the cheese factory, resulting in the production of 203,876 pounds of cheese. The cheese was sold primarily in Boston and New York, with the farmer receiving approximately 9¢ per pound. (Courtesy Town of DePeyster Historian.)

LEON KIRBY. Leon Kirby (1887–1965) works at the vats in the Royal Cheese Factory, located close to what is now known as Kokomo Corners. This was one of several cheese factories in the area. At the close of the Civil War, there was a marked increase in milk production, making it difficult for individual farmers to produce their own butter and cheese. This helped lead to the increase of the number of cheese factories in the area. (Courtesy Town of DePeyster Historian.)

MASONIC HALL. This building housed the DePeyster Masonic Lodge No. 573, which was instituted on July 4, 1865. Originally, the building that stood here was known as the Red Hall. It was the home of a wheelwright run by R. Ward. A building attached to this structure was used as a blacksmith shop, operated by Steff McBratney. The upper hall was used by the Masons fraternity as a gathering place and for social events. (Courtesy Town of DePeyster Historian.)

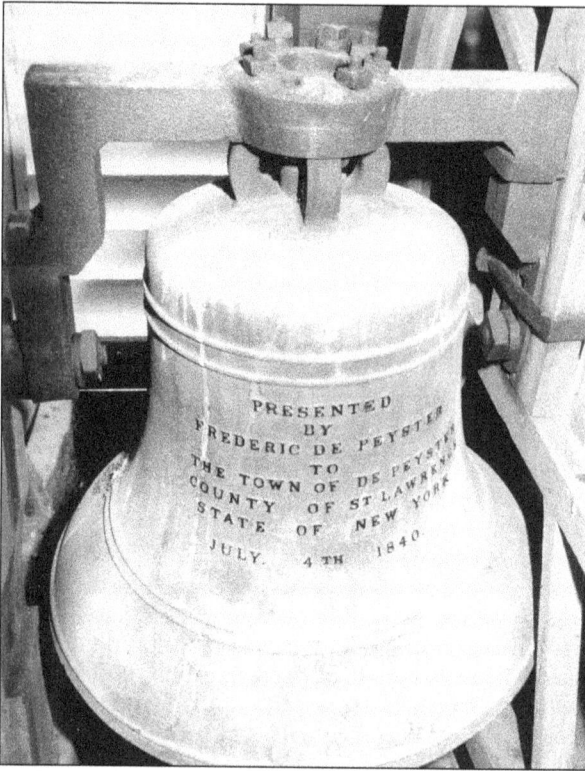

TOWN BELL. This bell was a gift from Frederick DePeyster in appreciation of having their name given to the new town back in 1825, when a portion of DeKalb and Oswegatchie were united to form the town of DePeyster. Until the town could find a place for the bell, it was hung in the tower of the Methodist church. It bears the inscription "Presented by Frederick DePeyster to the town of DePeyster, county of St. Lawrence, State of New York, July 4, 1840." (Courtesy Town of DePeyster Historian.)

METHODIST EPISCOPAL CHURCH. In 1827, members of the Methodist Episcopal church voted to incorporate a society. Since they had no building of their own, they met in the Bethal Union Church. In 1857, land was purchased and a new church was built to provide a space for regular worship. A spire of 105 feet was added in 1857, and in later years, other modifications were made to the structure that still stands today. It is interesting to note that the first Civil War rally in DePeyster took place in this church. (Courtesy Town of DePeyster Historian.)

METHODIST PARSONAGE. In the earliest days of rural communities, ministers would live with various church members (who took turns providing room and board) until proper housing became available. Here we see the parsonage for the Methodist Episcopal church, which was under construction on a piece of land purchased in 1857 for $500. (Courtesy Town of DePeyster Historian.)

MAIN STREET. This is an image facing south on Main Street in DePeyster. In this 1880 view we see, from left to right, the Methodist church, J. D. Wilson's store, the Conklin shop, the Mason House, the Congregational church, and the Johnson photo tent. It was not uncommon for itinerate as well as local photographers to set up a photo tent in an area where there was a major event taking place. (Courtesy Town of DePeyster Historian.)

FIRST CONGREGATIONAL CHURCH.
The Congregational church was built in 1860 at a cost of $5,000. It could seat up to 500 people. The Congregationalist Church Society was incorporated in 1858. The church was organized by Rev. W. Hulbert in 1822. There were originally 14 members. After it was incorporated, it was serviced by Reverend Dr. Francisco. This church was later purchased by the Grange in 1912 and used as a Grange until it burned in 1936. (Courtesy Town of DePeyster Historian.)

INTERIOR OF CONGREGATIONAL CHURCH. Pictured here is an interior view of the Congregational church in DePeyster. Apparently there was to be a memorial service for Pres. William McKinley. His picture is on display to the left. McKinley was the 25th president of the United States. He died on September 14, 1901, after being shot in Buffalo. (Courtesy Town of DePeyster Historian.)

LUDA WITHERELL. Luda Badger was born on a farm in DePeyster in 1881. Even as a young child, she had a desire to paint pictures. But life on a farm was hard, and there was little or no time for leisure activities, so her desire to paint had to be postponed until much later in her life. In 1905, she married Charles Witherell, pictured here with her. In 1946, she moved to Ogdensburg. In her declining years, she took up painting using leftover paint from a paint-by-numbers set. Luda painted what she saw in the world around her as well as from her own imagination, producing many fine works of art. She died in 1974. (Courtesy Town of DePeyster Historian.)

WITHERELL PAINTING. This painting of the Bethel Union Church was created by Luda Witherell. This old church was built in 1830 and torn down in 1896. The church was located in the general area of the present village park in DePeyster. The church was used by Presbyterians as well as Congregationalists and Universalists. Funds to build the church were provided by public and private donation. (Courtesy Town of DePeyster Historian.)

DePeyster School. This was DePeyster School District No. 1. Located on what is now county Route 10 in DePeyster, it was also known as the village school. The DePeyster school districts remained in use for 130 years before they were closed due to centralization. District No. 1 was built in the 1880s. In 1960, the district was sold, and the building is now a private home. (Courtesy Town of DePeyster Historian.)

School District No. 1. This was the school located on county Route 10 in DePeyster. From left to right are the following: (first row) Clifford Hazelton, Howard Young, Katherine Smithers, and Herbert Todd; (second row) Lois Hazelton, Jennie Cutway, Ada Young, Reginold Davison, and Mildred Lytle; (third row) Louie Cutway, Grace Witherell, Adeline Bogardus, Marjorie Mason, Lois Lytle, Winnifred Creighton, and Gerald Bogardus; (fourth row) Everette Todd, Lillian Todd, Sadie Rickett, Ruth Todd, Ben Lytle, Esther Giffin, and Merrill Putman. The teacher standing to the left is Rosco Mills. This picture was taken for the 1916–1917 school year. (Courtesy Town of DePeyster Historian.)

BOYS BASKETBALL. Competitive sports played a major role in entertainment before the advent of the electronic age. Not only schools but towns, villages, and various other organizations had their own teams. Here we see the Grange No. 1049 boys basketball team. From left to right are the following: (first row) Ralph Steele, Harve Badger, and Almon Smithers; (second row) Emery Smithers and Ralph Fishbeck. (Courtesy Town of DePeyster Historian.)

WOLOCOHELO GIRLS. The Wolocehelo Girls were associated with the Methodist church. *Wolocohelo* is a Native American word for work, loyalty, courage, and health. Seen here, from left to right, are the following: (first row) Mae Steele, Alice Kinney, Margaret Southern, Ruth Johnson, Lois Hazelton, and Mildred Lytle; (second row) Esther Giffen, Mrs. Southern, Nora Parks, End Wood, Grace Witherell, Lois Lytle, Carrie Poore, Sadie Blair, Dorothy Badger, June Conroy, Agnes Brown, Adah Young, Marjorie Mason, Adeline Bogardus, and Lillian Todd. (Courtesy Town of DePeyster Historian.)

KELLOGS CORNERS. During the War of 1812, when British troops invaded and captured the village of Ogdensburgh, residents of Ogdensburgh took refuge in an old tavern built at this location. In 1861, James Averill opened the town of DePeyster's first store here. This old barn was the original farmhouse on the Averill estate. (Courtesy Town of DePeyster Historian.)

GATES CURTIS. Gates Curtis was born on October 17, 1822, and was one of six children. At an early age, he demonstrated an aptitude for building things. In 1848, he established a foundry making plows and threshing machines in Bertheir, Canada. In 1855, he and his wife, Roxana J. Clement, returned to DePeyster and began farming. Twelve years later, he and his family moved to Ogdensburg. He is credited with the invention of several models of steel plows, a turbine waterwheel, and a shingle machine. Gates not only had mechanical interests but also had a passion for history. He wrote the definitive text *Our County and Its People: A Memorial Record of St. Lawrence County* in 1894. (Courtesy Town of DePeyster Historian.)

GEN. NEWTON MARTIN CURTIS.
Newton Martin Curtis was born on
May 21, 1835, a younger brother to
Gates Curtis, on a small farm in the
village of DePeyster in St. Lawrence
County. As a youth, he led a fairly
uneventful life. He attended local
schools and later became a teacher
and law student. When Fort Sumter
was attacked on April 12, 1861, he
felt the need to form a company of
men from the area and offer their
combined services to the Union
army. This group of 80 volunteers
became part of the 16th New York
Regiment. Newton Martin Curtis
led this regiment with the rank of
captain. Newton Curtis was involved
in many major battles, culminating
with the battle of Fort Fisher in North
Carolina, in which he was wounded
four times and awarded the Medal of
Honor for his deeds. (Courtesy Town
of DePeyster Historian.)

CURTIS CHILDREN. Newton Martin
Curtis married Emeline Clark and
they had six children, though one was
stillborn and another died 20 days after
birth. The four daughters who survived
are shown here in 1891. They are, from
left to right, Emma Phoebe, Mary Wroe,
Florence Rising, and Eliza Clark Curtis.
Emma married George Vilas in 1893.
She was the only daughter who married.
(Courtesy Town of DePeyster Historian.)

DEDICATION OF IOF HALL. This unique round timber-frame structure was built in 1896 for a new insurance organization called the Independent Order of Foresters (IOF). The unusual design was chosen by an amateur architect, who was also a local doctor in the village of DePeyster. The structure was later purchased by the Independent Order of Odd Fellows (IOOF), who made a number of modifications to the building. The dedication by the IOOF was a gala event. Most of the village turned out for the event, with flags flying and bands playing. (Courtesy DePeyster Historian.)

THE ROUND HALL. This unusual building is the only one of its kind in upstate New York and it still stands today. The roof is supported by a single pillar in the center of the building, leaving a large open space unobstructed by other pillars or beams. Now the property of the town of DePeyster, the building is used for numerous public functions, meetings, and provides office space for the town historian's office. (Courtesy Town of DePeyster Historian.)

DePeyster IOOF Band. This photograph was taken in 1918. From left to right are the following: (first row) Gerald Bogardus, P. A. Bogardus, Lysle Smithers, Lloyd Wilson, and Diamond Smithers; (second row) Gaylord Flectham, Jesse Lytle, Amias R. Thornton, Burdon W. Thornton, Charles Lytle, Charles Witherell, Harold Race, Arthur Youngs, Frank Breckenridge, Charles Flack of Heuvelton, and Prof. Vivian S. Thompkins. (Courtesy Town of DePeyster Historian.)

Off to War. Here we see a group of men preparing to board the train at Heuvelton. Seen here, from left to right, are Claude Preston Sr., Earl Sanderson, Harve Badger, Pat ?, John Todd, Claude Preston Jr., and Arlie Davison. These men were leaving to join the navy. (Courtesy Town of DePeyster Historian.)

NOAH PARISH. Noah Parish was born in DePeyster on November 20, 1890, and died in 1980. He lived all of his life in DePeyster. He was one of 21 men to go to World War I from the town. Parish was wounded twice in his military service. He suffered a hand grenade wound in Verdune and was severely wounded by machine gun fire on October 11, 1918, in the Argonne Forest. He was part of Company L, 327th Infantry Regiment. (Courtesy Town of DePeyster Historian.)

WALLACE ROCK. A resident of the town of DePeyster, Rock attended school in DePeyster and Heuvelton and worked on the farm of his uncle Herbert N. Holland. He enlisted in the U.S. Army Air Force at Pine Camp (now Fort Drum) on August 4, 1942. After training as a fighter pilot, Rock attained the rank of second lieutenant. He participated in the D-Day invasion and, after a number of missions, was reported missing on a flight over France. (Courtesy Marjorie Rock.)

ROBERT BRESETT. Robert Bresett, the son of Mr. and Mrs. W. J. Bresett, was a resident of DePeyster, attended high school in Heuvelton, and was inducted into the army on February 4, 1943. After basic training, he was sent to England in October 1943 and then to France on June 6 (D-Day). Bresett was a member of the 1st Army and fought in France, Belgium, and Germany. He was awarded the Purple Heart after being wounded. Later, he was reported killed in action in Belgium on December 19, 1943. (Courtesy Town of DePeyster Historian.)

WALTER WITHERELL. Walter Witherell was born on July 8, 1922, to James and Eliza Witherell of DePeyster. He graduated from Heuvelton High School in 1941. A graduate of the Potsdam Technical School, he entered the navy on October 12, 1942 and was assigned to Bomber Squadron BV 112. He was stationed at Port Layeute, North Africa, serving as a radar man and a waist gunner on a B-24 bomber. He was killed in action while on patrol in the Atlantic on November 30, 1943. (Courtesy Faye Witherell White.)

KOKOMO SCHOOL. Kokomo School District No. 4 was built by Luke Dean, Smith Stillwell, and Jonathan Fellows, who were the school commissioners of DePeyster in 1825. This replaced the former District No. 12 of Oswegatchie when a portion of the town of DePeyster was part of the township of Oswegatchie. The building was constructed by Thomas D. Witherell. By 1847, there were 50 children attending this school. In 1948, Kokomo became part of the Heuvelton Central School District. (Courtesy Town of DePeyster Historian.)

CLARINDA WILSON. Clarinda was born on January 7, 1809. She was the daughter of Thomas Wilson and Mercy Bristol. Mercy Bristol was the daughter of Samuel Bristol, who was the first known settler of DePeyster in 1802. Bristol opened a tavern near Mud Lake on State Road for use as an overnight rest stop. (Courtesy Town of DePeyster Historian.)

Three

LISBON

CHARLES E. TRACY. Charles Tracy stands in the doorway of his log cabin on Fulton Road in Lisbon after returning from the Civil War. The cabin was built by his grandfather Edward Kelly in the 1830s. Edward Kelly came to this country from Ireland and worked for Stephen VanRensselaer. In exchange for his labors, Kelly was given 40 acres of land. (Courtesy Eli Tracy.)

ADAM SCOTT. Adam Scott was born on September 21, 1817, at Bryantang, Ballynure, Ballytclere, County Antrim, Ireland. He was one of eight children and the second son of Adam and Ann McAllister Scott. He made the decision to come to America at a Belfast dock when he saw the wharves crowded with Irish farmers unloading corn raised in America to feed their families. From this sight Scott concluded that he would rather move to where he could grow his own food rather than having to buy it. (Courtesy Town of Oswegatchie Historian.)

SCOTT HOMESTEAD. Adam Scott immigrated to the village of Ogdensburg from Belfast, Ireland, and went to the home of Thomas Dollar, a second cousin. From there he went to work for James Ballantine. During his first year, he purchased 50 acres of land in the town of Lisbon. In the next 10 years, he added more than 100 acres of land to his farm. This house was the original 1850 structure, and it still stands today. (Courtesy Town of Oswegatchie Historian.)

TRACY HOMESTEAD. The cabin built by Edward Kelly was replaced by this fine home built in 1899 on the lot next door. This home stood for 31 years until it was destroyed by fire in 1920. From left to right are Leon Tracy, Ellan Agnus Kelly Tracy, Ralph Tracy (with his dog Zip), and Hazell Tracy England. (Courtesy Eli Tracy.)

CAPT. IRA OTIS TRACY. Ira Otis Tracy was born on September 17, 1858, in Lisbon. He was educated locally, including study at St. Lawrence University. He began the study of medicine, working in the offices of several local doctors. Tracy entered the College of Physicians and Surgeons in the autumn of 1880 and graduated with a degree in medicine in 1882. He entered military service and served in France, Siberia, and Russia. Upon returning to civilian life, he continued with general practice and psychiatry. He married Jennie E. Kelly on March 16, 1884. (Courtesy Eli Tracy.)

WINNING RED OXEN. Tractors were not common in the North Country, nor were they very reliable for those who had them. Most of the heavy work on the farm was done by oxen, which were generally mild-tempered and dependable. Here we see a pair of red oxen with Daniel L. Tracy at the St. Lawrence County Fair in Gouverneur, where they had won a pulling contest. Each of these animals weighed in at 2,000-plus pounds. (Courtesy Eli Tracy.)

EPISCOPAL CHURCH. This little church was built in 1856 from locally available fieldstone in the hamlet of Galloupville (later called Red Mills). Andrew O'Neill, one of the first settlers to the area, was a member of the church for many years. Lacking in priests as time went on, the church became less and less used, and the building was finally razed in 1963. (Courtesy Town of Lisbon Historian.)

ON THE HILL. This street in Lisbon is now known as Church Street (also previously known as "Back Street" by some citizens). On the right is St. Philip and James Catholic Church, built in 1884. Looking west down the street, we see the United Presbyterian Church and, in the distance, the spire of the Lisbon Wesleyan Church. (Courtesy Nancy J. LaFaver.)

THE WESLEYAN METHODIST CHURCH. This church had humble beginnings when it was organized on February 14, 1843, as the Lisbon Chapel. The chapel burned, and in 1878, the Lisbon Wesleyan Church was built at its current location. Livery stables and a parsonage were added as funds became available. (Courtesy Nancy J. LaFaver.)

ROBERT DAWLEY FARM. This early image of the Dawley residence in Lisbon was taken in 1900. Robert Dawley's father was born in Selby, Yorkshire, England, on July 12, 1816. His mother, Hanna Taylor Dawley, was born at Crickle House, Broughton, Yorkshire, England on July 16, 1824. The family immigrated to the United States and settled in Lisbon. (Courtesy Pat Fields.)

WILLIAM WOODSIDE. William Woodside was born in County Antrim, Ireland, and immigrated to America in July 1858. On November 24, 1863, he married Agnes Rea. He attended a Civil War rally in Lisbon, and all able-bodied men were asked to join. He enlisted in Elmira on December 9, 1863, and became a private in Company B Heavy Artillery. He was captured on May 12, 1864, at Spotsylvania and taken to Andersonville Prison, where his leg was seriously injured in a prisoner stampede. He was then transferred to Libby Prison and was later discharged from the service on June 28, 1865. (Courtesy Fran Doyle.)

THE 4-H FIRST ACHIEVEMENT PARADE. The Pine Grove 4-H club was one of the first 4-H Clubs in St. Lawrence County. This 4-H First Achievement event was held in Canton. The large banner reading, "Pine Grove 4-H Club" is from Lisbon. The club started around 1928 as an agriculture club. Shortly after its beginning, girls started to join. This picture was taken in front of Brewer Field House on the St. Lawrence University campus. (Courtesy Town of Lisbon Historian.)

THE BOICE HOMESTEAD. The Boice Homestead, which still stands on state Route 37 in Lisbon, was built in 1900 by Ellery Boice. The bricks for the house were made at the nearby Dawley farm since the Boices wanted to utilize as much locally made products as possible. Boice was working out west at the time, and Mary (Dawley) Boice had the house contracted and built to her specifications. The couple wanted to take advantage of the full St. Lawrence River view and had their home built with the largest windows available at that time. (Courtesy Town of Lisbon Historian.)

ART MAYNE. Pictured here is Art Mayne, owner of the Mayne Mill. This was a provender mill, providing feed for livestock. The office and mill were located in the former Lisbon Center House hotel. Mayne ran the mill for many years. It was later operated by Dewitt Aldrich. This photograph was taken for the 1930 Old Home Week celebration, which ran from August 17 to August 30. (Courtesy Eugene Jones.)

CHARLES "C. B." WRIGHT. Charles Wright is shown here sitting in his office at Wright's Feed Mill. This picture was taken for the 1930 Old Home Week in Lisbon. The mill took in local farmers' oats, ground them, and mixed them with barley and gluten to create animal feed. Wright also sold farm implements and supplies to area farmers. (Courtesy Eugene Jones.)

THE SHEFFIELD FARM MILK PLANT. The town and village of Lisbon are primarily agrarian communities, with milk being the main product. Nearly all the farmers in the town of Lisbon sent their milk to this plant for processing. The plant facility was previously used by the Doughnut Corporation, GLF, and lastly by Agway, which went out of business in the 1990s. (Courtesy Town of Lisbon Historian.)

THE KIT HOUSE. Around 1912, Smith G. and Emma Moore purchased this house as a kit from Montgomery Ward. The kit arrived in Lisbon on the train. The sections were picked up at the depot and brought to the construction site. The house was completed in 1914, and the stone porch was added later. There is another house on Main Street in Lisbon that has the same exact layout. It too was a Montgomery Ward house. (Courtesy Cathy and Mark Rusgrove.)

INTERNATIONAL TRACTOR. Here David LaRock is seen driving the tractor on the Samuel Livingston farm. Standing on the tractor is Menzo Johnson. David LaRock took his tractor and threshing machine to numerous farms to help farmers who did not have the equipment to harvest their crops. This picture was taken around 1940. (Courtesy Mary Lou Rupp.)

HOMER LIVINGSTON. It was not uncommon for people to have pets about the homestead, and sometimes these pets reflected the way the family made their living. In addition, it was not unusual for farmers to have large pets. Here we see Homer Livingston with a beautiful pair of white oxen that he kept on his farm on the Haggart Road. (Courtesy Mary Lou Rupp.)

OUT FOR A RIDE. What a way to remember days gone by—hitch up the horse, jump in the surrey, and go. This picture was taken in the 1940s on the Jay T. Livingston farm. In the front seat are Ruth Livingston (left) and Dorothy Livingston. In the back seat are Frank McRoberts (left) and his sister Gertrude McRoberts. (Courtesy Mary Lou Rupp.)

EARLY INTRODUCTIONS. Living and working on a farm made people respectful of the land and animals on which the farmers' livelihood depended. This photograph shows Mary Lou Simms (left) and her sister Barbara being introduced to a newborn calf. The picture was taken in 1959 on the William S. Simms farm on the Ogdensburg-Heuvelton Road. (Courtesy Mary Lou Rupp.)

NEVIN MEMORIAL CHURCH. The land for the Second Reformed Presbyterian Church of Lisbon was conveyed by James and Clarissa Martin on November 20, 1833. The church was also known as the "Town Line Church." In 1950, it was renamed the Nevin Memorial Church in memory of Rev. N. J. Nevin, who served as pastor for 29 years. (Courtesy Town of Lisbon Historian.)

ORIGINAL COVENANTER CHURCH. The original Covenanter Church (Reformed Presbyterian) was located on the corner of Cemetery and Tuck Roads in Lisbon. The church was formed in 1827, and this building was constructed in 1844. (Courtesy Town of Lisbon Historian.)

LISBON BASKETBALL TEAM. This is the Lisbon High School championship basketball team. From left to right are (first row) Eddie Scott, Bill Gray, Robert Mayne, Charles Moore, and Milford LeBarge; (second row) an unidentified coach, manager George Bush, Erwith Dezell, Don Harper, Donald Scott, Ken Robinson, Clarence Hill, Elwin Sprowls, and principal John Meckley. (Courtesy Town of Lisbon Historian.)

HEPBURN LIBRARY. Alonzo Barton Hepburn was born in the town of Colton on July 24, 1846. He served in the state government for a number of years and then entered the banking business. He accrued a huge fortune and, combining that with his love for education and the North Country, financed the construction of libraries in the towns of Colton, Edwards, Hermon, Lisbon, Madrid, Norfolk, and Waddington. This library in Lisbon opened on April 3, 1920. (Courtesy Town of Lisbon Historian.)

LISBON CENTER HOUSE. This hotel was constructed of locally procured stone in 1800 by Samuel Wells. Located on Main Street across from the railroad station, it was the ideal place for businessmen and visitors to stop and rest. The station had fine accommodations, including a small bar, writing rooms, and a fine dining room and kitchen. Livery services were also provided in a large barn to the rear of the hotel. (Courtesy Town of Lisbon Historian.)

RUNIONS BROTHERS PHOTOGRAPHY SHOP. This photography shop was located on Main Street in Lisbon. Brothers Alva J. and Charles E. Runions also had shops in Brasher Falls, Canton, Edwards, and Massena. (Courtesy Town of Lisbon Historian.)

DR. ERNEST E. THOMPSON. Dr. Ernest Thompson, wife Rosalind, and son David moved to Lisbon in 1935 and set up his medicine practice. During that time, he was the only physician in the area, serving Morley, Rensselaer Falls, and sometimes Heuvelton and DePeyster. Thompson was well known for his interest in his patients and became famous for making house calls in the winter either on skis or by snowplow. He also served on the staff of A. B. Hepburn Hospital and was president of the school board for many years. When he retired in 1977, he lived in Florida until his death in 1983. (Courtesy Ed Kight.)

ZOLLER GIRLS. This picture was taken in 1900. Here, sitting on their porch, are Gertrude Zoller (left) and her sister Francis Zoller. They were the daughters of Ivan and Fannie McRoberts Zoller. Gertrude later married Jay T. Livingston, and Francis married King David Livingston. (Courtesy Mary Lou Rupp.)

AT THE FAIR. Pictured here are Don Nelson (left) and Kara Russell at the Ogdensburg Fair sometime around 1912 or 1913. The Ogdensburg Fair, first opened in 1856, drew crowds from Lisbon, Morristown, DePeyster, Hammond, and even Canada. Lisbon 4-H groups were very active and had many exhibits at the fair. (Courtesy Town of Lisbon Historian.)

HUGH AND ELIZABETH JOHNSON.
Hugh Johnson was born on November
18, 1840, to John and Ann Wallace
Johnson, formerly of Ireland. Elizabeth
Ann Paterson Johnson was born on
December 17, 1844, at Woodford Farm
in Ogdensburg, owned by Henry Van
Rensselaer. Hugh Johnson served in the
Civil War and was wounded at Drewry's
Bluff, Virginia. On May 16, 1864, after
suffering a head wound, Johnson returned
to Ogdensburg and was asked by
Gen. Newton Martin Curtis to manage
the Curtis farm, which he did until he
was able to purchase his own farm in
DePeyster. (Courtesy Fran Doyle.)

BUSY STREET. This section of Main Street in Lisbon was by far the busiest part of the village.
Most of the products entering or leaving the village did so via the railroad. On the left is
the Center House, a major resting place for businessmen and visitors. Also in this area was
the railroad station as well as a number of stores and mills. (Courtesy St. Lawrence County
Historical Association.)

TOWN HALL. The original town hall was made from locally acquired stone in 1856 and, after approximately 33 years, was destroyed by fire. A new wooden structure was built in 1889. The new town hall served as a public meeting place for parties, town meetings, and various other social gatherings. The town hall suffered a fire that destroyed most of the records before 1882, but the building survived. (Courtesy Nancy LaFaver.)

RUTLAND STATION. The arrival of the railroad brought a burst of prosperity to the northern regions of St. Lawrence County. The Ogdensburg and Lake Champlain lines arrived in the Lisbon area around 1848, and the first station was built. Farm products such as cheese, milk, and butter could now be shipped to far markets, and a reverse flow of products as well as passenger service was established. The old station was destroyed by fire in 1925 and not rebuilt until 1927. In 1960, the railroad closed due to labor disputes and a marked decline in demand for rail services. (Courtesy Nancy LaFaver.)

Four

MORRISTOWN

MORRISTOWN FROM THE RIVER. This picturesque little village was located on the shore of the St. Lawrence River. As a result of the Macomb Purchase in 1787 and along with a series of purchases and other agreements, Governor Morris accumulated considerable land holdings in St. Lawrence County. The New York State legislature took a section of land from the town of Oswegatchie on March 7, 1821, and formed Morristown. The town was located directly across the river from what was Elizabethtown, Ontario (now called Brockville). (Author's collection.)

CIVIL WAR SOLDIERS MONUMENT. The monument seen here is standing in the center of the business district on Ford Street. Money for the monument was raised by the Woman's Relief Corps No. 84, an auxiliary to the Grand Army of the Republic (GAR), which raised money to care for disabled Civil War veterans. The monument was dedicated on May 30, 1911. The monument was later relocated to Chapman Village Park to make more room on the street for vehicular traffic in the business district. (Courtesy St. Lawrence County Historical Association.)

MAIN STREET. Today, Main Street is known as Ford Street. Running the entire length of the village, the business district can be found on the north end and residential homes on the south. Morristown contained some of the finest homes to be found in the northern part of the county. (Courtesy St. Lawrence County Historical Association.)

THE W. H. COMSTOCK COMPANY. The United States was flooded with proprietary remedies, and Dr. Morse's Indian Root Pills were no exception. Edwin Comstock founded W. H. Comstock Company in New York City, where it thrived until 1858. As a result of legal problems in the city, George and William H. Comstock moved the business to Brockville, Ontario, and the factory to Morristown in 1867. (Courtesy Verna Hutchinson.)

COMSTOCK EMPLOYEES. There was almost no major industry in this part of the county, so when Comstock moved in, the company instantly became the largest employer in the area. Although many men were employed here, most of the employees were women. Many of them spent all of their entire working years at Comstock, an unusual happening for the period. There were no minimum wage laws at this time. The women were paid $3 to $5 per week, and the men were paid $7 to $12. (Courtesy Verna Hutchinson.)

COMSTOCK'S DEAD SHOT PELLETS
FOR WORMS.

W. H. COMSTOCK, Sole Proprietor,
MORRISTOWN N. Y.

DEAD SHOT PELLETS. Trading cards such as this one were given to various druggists who handed them out to their patrons as a form of advertisement for the medications. The remedy advertised here was intended to treat numerous children's conditions and diseases, especially various types of worm infestations. The pellets contained substances such as turpentine, hemlock, linseed oil, and concentrated ammonia, but the company expounded the safety of the product. (Author's collection.)

Dr. MORSE'S INDIAN ROOT PILLS

W. H. COMSTOCK, Sole Proprietor,

DR. MORSE'S INDIAN ROOT PILLS. This trading card states the benefits of the root pills. The remedy was used to treat constipation, headache, kidney disease, neuralgia, foul breath, nervousness, jaundice, piles, dysentery, female complaints, and boils, to name a few. With the passage of the Food, Drug and Cosmetic Act in 1938, the company had to put the contents on the label, which included anise seed, black antimony, saltpeter, sulpher, hemlock oil, and often large amounts of sugar to kill the taste of the ingredients. (Author's collection.)

THE COMSTOCK INN. W. H. Comstock built a large inn between Main Street and Fitche's Bay, which opened into the St. Lawrence River. The inn was centrally located in the village and adjacent to the train station. A person could stay there for the sum of $2 a day. (Courtesy St. Lawrence County Historical Association.)

WHARF AND DEPOT. This view is looking down Morris Street toward the railroad depot and out over Fitche's Bay to Chapman's Point. The wharf was a major hub of activity for the village, with the railroad and river traffic coming together at the same location. (Courtesy St. Lawrence County Historical Association.)

MORRISTOWN AND BROCKVILLE FERRY. The first known ferry to cross the river on a regular basis was nothing more than a scow (a large flat-bottomed boat) built by Arnold Smith and Thomas Hill. Later, the first steamer, the *Indian Chief*, made regular runs. Here we see the *H. P. Bigelow* at the Morristown Wharf. The grain elevator to the right was operated by R. B. Chapman and Son. (Courtesy Verna Hutchinson.)

THE H. P. BIGELOW. The *Bigelow* was built in 1893 at Baldwinsville. It was 63 feet long and 14.25 feet abeam. It burned to the waterline at the Morristown dock in 1920. The remainder of its hull was sold to a company at Fort Regis, where it was rebuilt and used as a freight carrier. Here we see the *Bigelow* pulling away from the Morristown dock during its heyday. (Courtesy St. Lawrence County Historical Association.)

THE ISLAND BELLE. People living in riverside communities often took advantage of the many steamboats on the river. The steamer *Island Belle* and its sister ship, the *Riverside*, made regular runs between Clayton and Ogdensburg, stopping frequently in Morristown. Daily excursions were popular with religious groups and organizations of the time. Both steamers were owned by the Holmes brothers of Redwood. (Courtesy St. Lawrence County Historical Association.)

THE ELMER W. JONES. This ferry was built in Groton, Connecticut, and was serving well at Morristown. But during World War II, the craft was requisitioned by the U.S. Navy and sent to Staten Island to serve in the war effort. In 1946, it was released from naval service and returned to Morristown, where previous duties were continued until it made its last trip, on December 7, 1952. (Author's collection.)

PRESBYTERIAN CHURCH. This church was organized in 1822, but it was not until 1837–1838 that the congregation had a building of its own. The house of worship was built on Gouverneur Street on property donated by the Chapman family. The church was built in the Georgian style with stately columns in the front of the structure with materials donated by the parishioners, who also bought pews for their families to use in order to help raise money for the structure. To encourage worshipers to come from outside the village, carriage sheds were built behind the church. (Courtesy St. Lawrence County Historical Association.)

THE METHODIST AND CATHOLIC CHURCHES. The Methodist church in Morristown was organized in 1843. They built their first church building in 1848, and it was destroyed by fire in 1850. In 1851, a new brick structure was constructed. The new church contained six stained-glass windows by Harry J. Horwood, a stained-glass artist from Ogdensburg. The first services in St. John's Catholic Church, seen here on the right, were held on December 23, 1878. A parochial school was started in 1949 for grades one through six. The classes were taught by the Sisters of St. Joseph from Watertown. The school was closed in 1969. (Courtesy St. Lawrence County Historical Association.)

INGHAM CHURCH. Also known as the Chippewa Street Congregational Church of Brier Hill and locally known as the Ingham Church. This church was organized in 1827 with nine members and Rev. Hiram Johnson as its first pastor. Most of the land and money to build the church was provided by John Ingham. (Courtesy St. Lawrence County Historical Association.)

PUBLIC SCHOOL. In 1876, the Morristown Union Free School was organized and implemented with the involvement of a number of prominent citizens on the board of education: Harry Hooper (president), J. Garvin, M.D. (clerk), C. F. Yennie, T. D. Losee, A. F. Carpenter, A. Proctor, Harry Russell, E. Kingsland, and Frank Chapman. (Courtesy St. Lawrence County Historical Association.)

BRIDGE ACROSS THE BAY. Morristown was born on March 27, 1821, by appropriating land from the town of Oswegatchie. Chippewa Creek (also known as "Jibway," meaning "swamp") bisected the new village. The creek opens into a bay that, in turn, empties into the St. Lawrence River. To make lands available on both sides of the creek, a small wooden bridge was built. Although it has been modified several times, it is still in use today. (Courtesy Verna Hutchinson.)

RAILROAD STATION AND WHARF. The first railroad to reach Morristown was the Rome, Watertown and Ogdensburg. This line was followed by the New York Central. The tracks ran along the river. At Morristown, they ran between the buildings of the W. H. Comstock Company, which was the largest shipper in the area. The station was near the Comstock Inn and the wharf. Later a turntable was located here to allow train cars to be loaded onto the Armstrong (a ferry designed to carry railroad cars) for transport to Canada. (Courtesy St. Lawrence County Historical Association.)

THE OLD WINDMILL. Morristown had little or no waterpower most of the time, as the St. Lawrence River was too slow to be useful. But there was plenty of wind. In 1825, a Scotsman named Hugh McConnell built a windmill on an elevated portion of the town. McConnell was one of the earliest Scottish settlers in the area and, being a miller himself, operated the mill until he accidentally drowned in 1826. The windmill was soon shut down and abandoned, but the stone portion of the mill still stands. It remains the only mill of its kind ever built in this area. (Author's collection.)

THE OLD WINDMILL. MOrristown.

CHAPMAN RESIDENCE. Originally known as the Ford Mansion, this stately home was built by Jacob Ford (a member of the Ford family). It was located on a piece of land known as Barnard's Point (later named Chapman's Point), which extended out into the St. Lawrence River in Morristown. The mansion resembles another Ford family home built in Morristown, New Jersey. The mansion later contained an artist studio where the famous artist Charles Chapman painted. (Author's collection.)

VILLAGE LIBRARY. Richard B. Chapman took over the family business in Morristown from his father, Augustus Chapman. Chapman and Company had a small land office located in a stone building on Main Street in Morristown. This building was later donated by the Chapmans to the town to be used as a public library. To this day, it remains as the town's library. (Courtesy Verna Hutchinson.)

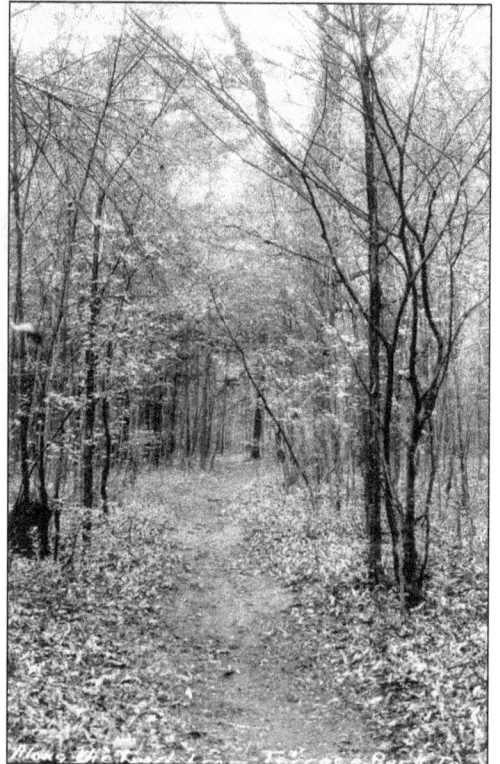

WOODED TRAIL. In the latter half of the 1870s, St. Lawrence County was still quite heavily wooded. There was approximately one mile between the village of Morristown and Terrace Park. Roads were still not much more than trails, and there was little vehicular traffic. This is a walking path between Terrace Park and Morristown. (Courtesy Marjorie Rock.)

TERRACE PARK CABINS. In the spring of 1874, a group of businessmen from Oswegatchie and surrounding towns arrived on the steamer *Henry Plumb* for a picnic with their families on an elevated area at the water's edge just west of Morristown. Liking the area, they decided to purchase it and form the St. Lawrence International Campground Association. They built many fine cabins and cottages (as shown here) to encourage visitors. They also provided tents for the less affluent guests. (Courtesy St. Lawrence County Historical Association.)

BOARDWALKS. The St. Lawrence International Campground Association was later named Terrace Park. The landscape around Terrace Park was hilly and uneven, making walking difficult for guests. Boarded walkways were laid down between cottages, and a fine hotel was also built there in 1882. At the turn of the century, the hotel and several cottages were destroyed by fire, and the glory of Terrace Park rapidly faded. (Courtesy St. Lawrence County Historical Association.)

TERRACE PARK BAY. Most of the guests at Terrace Park arrived by steamer or train. There were daily trains from Ogdensburg to Morristown and back, as well as numerous steamboats that arrived at a pier built for the park. Steamers and trains arrived at Terrace Park Bay, but the guests had to climb a long and steep stairway to get up to the park.

GRAND ARMY OF THE REPUBLIC. At the close of the Civil War, some local veterans organized the Alfred I. Hooker Post No. 414. This group organized in 1883 with John LaVigne as one of its commanders. LaVigne also oversaw the operation of the plush Terrace Park Hotel and was partly responsible for the Grand Army of the Republic (GAR) holding its reunions here for many years. (Courtesy St. Lawrence County Historical Association.)

BRIER HILL. The hamlet of Brier Hill in Morristown is somewhat centrally located in the town on what is now known as state Route 37. The community has always been a rural agrarian community with a lack of major industry. The first post office was established in 1853, and the first postmaster was David Giffin. There were a number of stores as well as a cheese factory, but otherwise the community was residential. Pictured here are Matt Stevenson and his family out for a ride in his new Buick. (Courtesy St. Lawrence County Historical Association.)

BRIER HILL STATION. The railroad first came to Brier Hill in 1876. Brier Hill now had a direct connection to Watertown in the west and Ogdensburg to the east. The railroad was first provided by the Rome, Watertown and Ogdensburg Railroad and later by the New York Central line. Although transportation and shipping was now more convenient and economical, there was no great prosperity derived by the railway. (Courtesy St. Lawrence County Historical Association.)

BRIER HILL SCHOOL. The first schoolhouse built in the Brier Hill area was constructed on the corner of Olds Mill Road. A new building was built for a school on Main Street in Brier Hill in 1871. The building became inadequate and was moved to Elm Street. A second story was added to the building in 1895. The school continued to be used until 1944, when it was finally closed due to centralization of local schools. (Courtesy Verna Hutchinson.)

ELM STREET. This quiet residential street was probably first opened shortly after 1904, when the Young Memorial Church was built. The street was originally called Elm Street but is now known as School Street. The two fine homes pictured here are now gone, but the Young Memorial Church (the stone structure) can be seen here from the rear. The front of the church faces interstate Route 37. (Courtesy St. Lawrence County Historical Association.)

THE JOHN INGHAM HOUSE. This stone house was built in 1835 by John Ingham and located about two miles from Brier Hill. This beautiful home was constructed of local fieldstone. As farmers cleared their fields for planting, the fencerows were soon piled high with stone, which proved to be an excellent building material. The house had a fireplace at each end of the house, a number of built-in bookcases, and exterior green slat shutters on the windows. (Courtesy Verna Hutchinson.)

ROLLWAY HOTEL. The Rollway Hotel was built on the south side of Black Lake by a game protector named John Gaddis. The hotel was used mainly as a halfway house by traveling men and the public. The name Rollway came from a geological feature that allowed logs to be rolled into Fish Creek and then to Pope's Mills. (Courtesy St. Lawrence County Historical Association.)

MAIN STREET, BRIER HILL. This photograph of Brier Hill was taken around 1906. The building to the immediate right is the Odd Fellows Hall. The third building from the right was originally a large barn on the corner that was remodeled into a store. (The barn, moved up from the depot, was once a sash and blind factory.) The building later served as a post office, grocery, and telephone exchange. (Courtesy St. Lawrence County Historical Association.)

MAIN STREET, HAMMOND. Established on March 30, 1827, Hammond got its name from Abijah Hammond of New York, who owned the township previous to 1814. On September 12, 1914, David Parish purchased a large portion of the area from Hammond. No industry developed in this area, and it was always a farming community. In this image, we see part of the business district in the village of Hammond in the early 1900s. State Route 37 runs through the village. Black Lake Road intersects Route 37 and continues on to interstate Route 12. (Courtesy St. Lawrence County Historical Association.)

MILL STREET, HAMMOND. In this view of Mill Street, looking east, we see on the immediate left the Burt C. Jones residence, built by William Soper in 1902. Stephen (left) and Clinton Jones are standing on the porch. The next two houses down are the Marshall Soper residence and the David McCadam residence. (Courtesy St. Lawrence County Historical Association.)

RED BRICK TAVERN. This old tavern was apparently built by Abner Swain around 1811 in what is now Main Street in Brier Hill. The tavern was a stagecoach stop on the Ogdensburg-Utica route, and at that time most of the roads were plank roads. The tavern had 20 rooms as well as a large ballroom for local events. There were quarters for servants and a room set aside for the weaving of cloth. Behind the tavern were spacious accommodations for horses and buggies. (Courtesy Verna Hutchinson.)

STORE-SCHOOLHOUSE, MORRISTOWN. George Couper moved to Morristown from Perth Ontario in 1818 and began teaching school. Around 1824, a stone schoolhouse was built on Columbia Street and became District No. 1. The school was heated with a small box stove using wood provided by students' parents as partial payment for the schooling. Teachers' salaries were $3 per day, and they would board with various families. Attendance was not mandatory, and the older boys would often drop out seasonally to help with planting and harvesting. (Courtesy Verna Hutchinson.)

BRIER HILL STORE. There were two stores in Brier Hill. Pictured is Matt Stevenson with his new Buick in front of his store. Immediately to the left of the car is Dr. Fred E. Graves. Alsworth "Olie" Giffin is standing at the left on the top step. This picture was taken around 1909. (Courtesy St. Lawrence County Historical Association.)

YOUNG MEMORIAL CHURCH. During the spring of 1904, Enoch Young and sisters Jeanette and Elizabeth offered to provide a plot of land in the hamlet of Brier Hill to build a church. In the spring of 1905, work started on the foundation. S. D. P. Williams, architect of Ogdensburg, presented the spade for turning the first scoop of earth. Lumber and timbers were cut and milled locally. The cornerstone was laid in June 1907. The windows were executed by H. J. Horwood, stained-glass artist of Ogdensburg. (Courtesy St. Lawrence County Historical Association.)

UNION CHURCH AND CEMETERY. The first church to be built in Brier Hill was the Union Church, established in 1859. The church remained viable until 1925, when it was sold to be used as a farm and radio supply store. The old church still stands but would be hard to recognize, since it is being used as a garage. The cemetery is still well kept. (Courtesy St. Lawrence County Historical Association.)

CHAMBER'S STORE. This store was built at the junction of Black Lake Road and Route 58 by Welch and Rogers of Hammond. They rented it to W. O. Chambers, who sold groceries, dry goods, furniture, and harnesses. (Courtesy St. Lawrence County Historical Association.)

LOGGING IN MORRISTOWN. Throughout most of the North Country, logging was a major industry. The countryside was covered with great stands of the finest oak and maple. Elm, needed for making cheese boxes, was plentiful, as was as mountain ash.

PERRY HOTEL. Located on Black Lake just south of Morristown is the hamlet of Edwardsville, also referred to as "the Narrows" (in reference to its location on the lake). It was here that Henry Perry purchases a piece of land from the Polhman family and erected a grand Hotel referred to as Perry's Hotel or the Black Lake House. The hotel was four stories high and had a grand ballroom that was used for social events and other gatherings. (Courtesy Verna Hutchinson.)

PERRY HOTEL GUESTS. The Perry Hotel became a mecca, drawing tourists from all over the state during the summer and the winter months. The Allen Stock Company came to the hotel every summer for several years, presenting plays for guests and locals alike. There were parties and dances in the ballroom, and silent movies were also shown. In the winter months, there were skating parties on the lake. Here we see a group of guests preparing to take a hayride. (Courtesy Verna Hutchinson.)

EDWARDSVILLE FERRY. Henry Ellenwood established the first regular ferry at Edwardsville in 1851. It consisted of a flat-bottomed boat with a cable that a man was able to pull himself to the island (now known as Booth's Island). From there another ferry would take passengers the rest of the way to the mainland in the town of DePeyster. Eventually, the ferry became large enough to carry automobiles. This service came to an end in 1902 with the building of a wooden bridge. (Courtesy Verna Hutchinson.)

OLD BLACK LAKE ROAD. When the Native Americans traveled from one place to another, they usually took the path of least resistance. The route they took from Ogdensburg through the Black Lake area was often followed and became the first road through the area. Known as the Black Lake Road, this section above Edwardsville is not much better than a path. It remained this way until the advent of the automobile. (Courtesy St. Lawrence County Historical Association.)

Five

RENSSELAER FALLS

MILBURN WAGONS. Milburn Wagons was one of two wagon shops in the village of Rensselaer Falls. Located near the train depot, between the tracks and the Oswegatchie River, they handled all sorts of buckboards, manure wagons, buggies, and surreys. The two tracks leading out of the upper story were used to push wagons up to the second story, where they were stored. (Courtesy Village of Rensselaer Falls Historian.)

OFF TO THE FAIR. The county fair was originally located in Ogdensburg in 1856. As Ogdensburg is located in the northern part of the county, a trip there was a time-consuming event. With the advent of the railroad in Rensselaer Falls in 1862, the trip was no longer a problem. Here we see a group of people boarding the train at Rensselaer Falls for the fair in Ogdensburg. (Courtesy Verna Hutchinson.)

LOADING CHEESE AT THE STATION. As dairy herds increased, so did milk production. More milk was produced than could be consumed locally. As a result, cheese factories became quite prevalent. The railroad became a major benefit to the cheese industry as a means of shipping the product to distant markets. At this railroad station, cheese is loaded on cars and shipped to Boston, New York City, and locations throughout the state. (Courtesy St. Lawrence County Historical Association.)

110

OTIS T. CRANE. Without a doubt, the railroad was by far the most important factor in the development of rural communities. Everyone would benefit in some way, especially the thousands of people who had jobs because of the railroad. Here we see Otis T. Crane, the station agent for the New York Central Railroad from 1898 to 1946. (Courtesy Village of Rensselaer Falls Historian.)

RENSSELAER FALLS DEPOT. When first arriving in Rensselaer Falls, the railroad was a branch of the road between Norwood and Watertown. In 1862, more track was laid down, and the line continued on to Ogdensburg. (Courtesy Village of Rensselaer Falls Historian.)

RENSSELAER FALLS DEPOT. A depot was built in 1862, and the Rome, Watertown and Ogdensburg Railroad provided services that eventually led to several trains each day for passengers and freights. The railroad was eventually replaced by the New York Central line, which continued to operate until 1954, when the station was finally closed after services had reduced to a trickle and then ceased altogether. The tracks were finally pulled from the railroad bed and sold for salvage. (Courtesy Verna Hutchinson.)

PLOWING SNOW. North Country snowstorms could dump as much as two to three feet of snow in a day. With the high winds and drifting, transportation would come to a standstill. The plow shown here is pushed by two engines of the New York Central line in 1908 to clear the tracks. State and town roads were often closed during such storms, and the railroad was the only means to get from one town to another. (Courtesy Verna Hutchinson.)

METHODIST CHURCH. In 1853, the Methodist church was organized. Having no building to worship in, the congregation used the village school led by Rev. Almanzo Blackman. In 1858, they built their own church in Pioneer Park. In 1867, the church had outgrown the old structure, so it was sold and moved to a new space. A new brick structure was built on the location. (Courtesy Verna Hutchinson.)

CONGREGATIONAL CHURCH. The Congregational Church of Rensselaer Falls was first organized on June 6, 1842. The first church building was completed in 1848 and was dedicated on January 11, 1849. In 1954, the Methodist and Congregational churches united to form the United Church of Rensselaer Falls. The old Congregational church is no longer in use and hopefully will be the new home of the Rensselaer Falls Historical Association. (Courtesy Verna Hutchinson.)

CREIGHTON'S HALL. Formally known as the Grange Hall, this building was located on Rensselaer Street next to the Congregational church. Used for public gatherings and recreation, the building had a poolroom as well as an ice-cream parlor in the front of the structure.

N. A. Bockus. Gen'l Store   Rensselaer Falls. N.Y.

N. A. BOCKUS GENERAL STORE. The Bockus hardware store was located next to the tracks on Front Street, not far from the depot. Any item needed by farm or village was available here—items such as Ruberoid roofing materials, washing machines, grinding stones of all kinds, implements for digging and cutting, clothing, shoes, boots, and furniture. An undertaking parlor was housed at one end of the building, with coffins in stock or made to order. (Courtesy Verna Hutchinson.)

Rensselaer Falls Mill. On this location in 1842, Henry Van Rensselaer charged John Shull Sr. to build a gristmill for the village. On a number of occasions, the mill burned or was damaged by floods but was rebuilt each time and with added improvements. A previous stone mill burned in 1913, and the present mill was built in 1914. (Courtesy Verna Hutchinson.)

Main Street, Rensselaer Falls. This picture was taken sometime after 1936, when concrete was laid in the road. Down the street can be seen the new iron bridge that spans the canal and the Oswegatchie River. The tall building to the left is the library, followed by McBride's Mercantile, the IGA store, and the Masonic Hall. (Courtesy Village of Rensselaer Falls Historian.)

RENSSELAER STREET, NORTH. This view of Rensselaer Street shows, from left to right, J. J. Doty's, the Masonic Hall, Charlie Parson's, Simpson's, the Library Building, and a dry goods store. Farther down the street on the left is Creighton's Hall and the Congregational church. (Courtesy St. Lawrence County Historical Association.)

RENSSELAER STREET, SOUTH. Like every community large and small, Rensselaer Falls has had its share of disastrous fires. Two major fires (one in 1903 and the other in 1954) destroyed a good part of the business district seen here on the left. There were fires involving the school and most of the mills along the river. There was little or no firefighting equipment. A fire department was finally organized in 1923, but it still had no equipment. (Courtesy St. Lawrence County Historical Association.)

116

NEW IRON BRIDGE. This iron bridge was built in 1895 to replace the old wooden bridge. The new bridge was wider with walkways on both sides for pedestrian traffic. The wooden deck was removed and replaced with cement in 1930, providing a longer-lasting surface. The concrete surface was removed in 1988 to reduce weight and was paved over with asphalt. (Courtesy Verna Hutchinson.)

THE RIVERSIDE HOTEL. This hotel was built by M. W. Spaulding in the early years of the village and was later known as Charles Chapin's Hotel. The hotel had a large hall for shows and dances. It was also used by the Masons for several years as a meeting place. (Courtesy Village of Rensselaer Falls Historian.)

LOGGING AT THE FALLS. The lumber industry was of major importance to Rensselaer Falls from its earliest days. Logs were floated down the Oswegatchie River to the mills in the summer months, but in the winter more hands were freed up from working in the fields, so more men were able to help cut trees from otherwise inaccessible areas and pull them over the frozen ground on heavy-duty sleighs pulled by workhorses. (Courtesy Village of Rensselaer Falls Historian.)

BOX FACTORY. The box factory can be seen here on the shore of the Oswegatchie River. Rensselaer Falls was at the perfect location for the operation of several mills, one of which was the box factory. At this location, there was a drop of approximately six feet in the river elevation. This drop provided the kinetic energy to power the mills. Logs were floated downstream and stored near the mill. The logs were then drawn up into the mill, debarked, and made into cheese boxes. (Courtesy Verna Hutchinson.)

118

CHEESE BOX FACTORY. This mill was originally used by the Phoenix Bent Works but, in 1880, was converted into the production of cheese boxes. Now that there were numerous cheese factories in the town of Rensselaer Falls and the surrounding towns, a readily available supply of shipping boxes was necessary. Under the direction of B. F. Spooner, this factory was producing 1,000 cheese boxes a day. (Courtesy Verna Hutchinson.)

WORKERS AT THE BOX FACTORY. Workers pictured here are, from left to right, as follows: (first row) Ray Madill; (second row) William Charlton, William VanWaters, Charles Leonard, Alva Dickinson (seated in front of Leonard), John Crawford, William Blair, Henry Parkell, Frank Crary, Bert Morris, William Dart, Amos Bockus, William Spry, and Enoch Harvey; (third row) John Jesmer, Fred Crawford, Lynn Sims, Carl Randall, Fernando Roca, Lewis Spry, Frank Moore Jr., Neil Hanson, Ed Lee, Joe Randall, and Lorne Jenkins. (Courtesy Verna Hutchinson.)

T. M. McKelvey Store. This old store was located just over the tracks near the train station and across from the N. A. Bockus hardware store. The building housed the T. M. McKelvey dry goods and grocery store and the C. W. Lent store. The second floor of the building housed the milliner J. R. Gilbert. The building was destroyed by fire in 1900, and the S. J. Orr harness shop and livery was built on the site. (Courtesy Village of Rensselaer Falls Historian.)

N. A. Bockus Furniture Parlors. It was common practice for furniture makers to also make coffins, as both were usually constructed in the same shop in the back of the stores. In this picture, a coffin is on display in the front of the undertaking parlor on the left. From left to right are N. A. Bockus, Tom McKelvey, Jud Gutterson (on the hearse), and Fred Bockus. (Courtesy Village of Rensselaer Falls Historian.)

ITINERANT PEDDLER. Much of the population in the townships was rural. Farm life was hard and usually required all of the daylight hours for chores, and there was little or no time for anything else. Travel to and from business centers was too costly in time and effort to be done on a daily basis, so peddlers would travel the streets of the towns and rural roads to peddle wares needed for daily use. This peddler standing next to his wagon full of wares is believed to be Julius Wohlfarth. (Courtesy Village of Rensselaer Falls Historian.)

VILLAGE OF RENSSELAER FALLS. Rensselaer Falls is tucked away in the northwest corner of the town of Canton, in close proximity to the towns of Oswegatchie, DePeyster, Lisbon, and DeKalb. The town was originally named Tateville after Robert Tate, a surveyor and prominent citizen. It was also known as Canton Falls before the establishment of the first post office there in 1851, with Archibald Shull as the first postmaster. (Courtesy Village of Rensselaer Falls Historian.)

BENIAH AND EUNICE MORRISON. Beniah Morrison was born in 1818 in Straksborough, Addison County, Vermont. He was the eldest of four boys and three girls. In 1844, after the death of his father, he came to St. Lawrence County and settled in what is now known as Rensselaer Falls. In 1841, he married Eunice Millington, and they had three children—Benjamin F., Edna H., and Leroy. (Courtesy Village of Rensselaer Falls Historian.)

MORRISON FARM. After arriving in Rensselaer Falls, Beniah Morrison purchased 25 acres of land and went into the nursery business. He continued to purchase land until he had 365 acres of land. His nursery business flourished, and he was soon producing seedlings by the thousands. He not only grew trees but also produced some very fine cattle. (Courtesy Village of Rensselaer Falls Historian.)

122

COMMERCIAL HOUSE. This building was built in 1852 by Henry VanRensselaer. In 1903, the structure was destroyed by a fire that started in the rear of the building and soon spread to other nearby buildings. Soon Hinsdale's Store, a small office building, and a barn of the Mckee residence were destroyed. (Courtesy Village of Rensselaer Falls Historian.)

NEW BUILDING. After the destruction of the old commercial house by fire in 1903, a new brick building was built using the foundation of the previous building. The southwest corner of the building contained the post office and remained there for many years. Two of the early postmistresses were Myron Jenkins and Jesse McBride. The building also housed a few small stores and later the fire company. (Courtesy Village of Rensselaer Falls Historian.)

ICE HARVESTING. During the winter months, every available hand was necessary for the ice harvest. After the ice in the Oswegatchie River reached a certain thickness, men would take a large, one-man saw and cut blocks of ice just big enough for one man to handle. Other men using a long pole called a pike and large iron tongs would loosen the blocks for harvesting. (Courtesy Village of Rensselaer Falls Historian.)

ICE HARVESTING. Loose blocks of ice were pushed and pulled up ramps onto flatbed sleighs and then stacked. The horse-drawn sleighs were then drawn to icehouses, where the blocks of ice were stacked by the cord and then buried in sawdust. The sawdust was an excellent insulator and would keep the ice from melting through the warmer months. Thus there would be plenty of ice for refrigeration. (Courtesy Village of Rensselaer Falls Historian.)

LITTLE RED SCHOOL HOUSE. A small one-room schoolhouse was built in 1850 on the corner of State and Main Streets, and apparently was the second school built in the town. The school was moved in 1862 and converted to a private residence. This two-room school was constructed on the same location. The two-room school was replaced by a two-story building in 1882. (Courtesy Village of Rensselaer Falls Historian.)

HIGH SCHOOL. The Union Free School was destroyed by fire on February 3, 1903. A new school building was designed by James P. Johnston and S. D. P. Williams from Ogdensburg. James Johnston designed many fine homes and public buildings throughout the state and in New York City. The new school building had five classrooms and a library. (Courtesy Village of Rensselaer Falls Historian.)

THE 1930–1931 CHAMPS. The Rensselaer Falls high school competed with many area schools and won their share of the games. Shown here, from left to right, are (first row) Lloyd Jenkins, Walter Hering, Wayne Seaman, Glenn Perry, and Prof. John Sweet; (second row) Barry Graham, Roy MacMonogle, Lawrence Glidden, Clarence Perry, and Bert Perry. (Courtesy Village of Rensselaer Falls Historian.)

BOYS BASEBALL TEAM. This group represents the Rensselaer Falls boys baseball team. The local teams competed against other schools and earned their share of wins. Shown, from left to right, are the following: (first row) Howard Jenkins, Kenneth Seaman, Allan Jenkins, Maurice MacMonagle, Lloyd Jenkins, and Loren McAdoo; (second row) Leo Burke, Hobart Springs, Kenneth Ginn, Wendell VanDyke, Lowell England, and Ivan Breaky. (Courtesy Village of Rensselaer Falls Historian.)

HIGH SCHOOL TEAM. This group of students represents Rensselaer Falls High School for 1921. From left to right are the following: (first row) Dorothy Woodcock, Dorothy Ginn, Ruth VanDyke, Dorothy VanDyke, and Mildred Dexter; (second row) Lorne McAdoo, Harry Wainwright, Allen Jenkins, Maurice MacMonagle, Lloyd Jenkins, and Kenneth Seaman. (Courtesy Village of Rensselaer Falls Historian.)

THE 1932–1933 GIRLS BASKETBALL TEAM. Pictured here is the high school girls basketball team from Rensselaer Falls. From left to right are the following: (first row) Alma Jenkins, Elizabeth Sullivan, Ada Reidell, Anita MacMonagle, Leona Wilson, Kathleen Carpenter, and Ruth Pratt; (second row) Ruth Billings (teacher), Genevive Besio, Grace Sizeland, Harriet Stirpe, Edith Herne, and Stanley Hicks (principal). (Courtesy Village of Rensselaer Falls Historian.)

GIRLS HIGH SCHOOL BASKETBALL. This is the 1928–1929 girls basketball team from Rensselaer Falls High School. From left to right are the following: (first row) Leona Backus, Eileen Jenkins, Gladys Grimshaw, Louise Pratt, and Anita MacMonagle; (second row) Jean Heatherington, Hazel Griffiths, Prof. John Sweet, Velma Cleland, and Armaminta Blair. (Courtesy Village of Rensselaer Falls Historian.)

EARLY BASEBALL TEAM. Before the age of electronics, entertainment was primarily found locally. America's game—baseball—became one of the first to develop. Here we see a very early team for the village of Rensselaer Falls. From left to right are the following: (first row) Chester Wainwright, Myron Jenkins, Lorne Jenkins, and Hank Backus; (second row) Elmer Jenkins, S. McAllister, Frank Moore, and Pete England; (third row) Charles Leonard, Fred Burk, William Perry, and unidentified. (Courtesy Village of Rensselaer Historian.)

www.ingramcontent.com/pod-product-compliance
Lightning Source LLC
Chambersburg PA
CBHW080552110426
42813CB00006B/1287